© 2018 John O. Gooch, Ph.D.

John O. Gooch, Ph.D.
Playing With the Big Kids: Central Methodist University 1982-2016

All rights reserved.

No part of this publication may be reproduced, stored in a retrieval system or transmitted in any form or by any means, electronic, mechanical, photocopying, recording or otherwise without the prior permission of the author or in accordance with the provisions of the Copyright, Designs and Patents Act 1988 or under the terms of any license permitting limited copying issued by the Copyright Licensing Agency.

Published by: Eagle Heights Press

Edited by: Delia Remington

ISBN-10: 1-947181-04-5

ISBN-13: 978-1-947181-04-5

Distributed by:
Eagle Heights Press
414 N. Church St.
Fayette, MO 65248

John O. Gooch, Ph.D.

PLAYING WITH THE BIG KIDS
CENTRAL METHODIST UNIVERSITY
1982-2016

Eagle Heights Press
Fayette, MO

OTHER BOOKS BY JOHN GOOCH

John Wesley for the 21st Century

Circuit Riders to Crusades:
Essays in Missouri Methodist History

Being a Christian in the Wesleyan Tradition

Claiming the Name: A Theological and Practical
Overview of Confirmation

103 Questions Youth Workers Ask

Playing With The Big Kids

Central Methodist University
1982-2016

JOHN O. GOOCH, PH.D.

Table of Contents

Introduction
Time Line
1. The World of Education
2. A New Day Dawns
3. Transforming the Board of Curators
4. Transforming Finances
5. Transforming the Campus
6. Celebrating a Sesquicentennial
7. Transforming the Curriculum
8. The College of Graduate and Extended Studies
9. We Become a University
10. Transforming Student Success
11. Transforming Student Life
12. Transforming the Alumni Association
13. What is Christian Higher Education?
14. Central Methodist and the Church
15. Transforming Students
16. Transition to the Future

INTRODUCTION

This is a book about transformation, OR how a sleepy little college in a sleepy little town in rural Missouri became a university. So, what is transformation? My dictionary says that to transform is "to change in structure, appearance, or character."[1] To change in structure is what institutions often do when they don't know what else to do. If they are in decline, and they aren't sure what to do about it, they re-structure, often ignoring the real issues. To change in appearance is often superficial. Cinderella's fairy godmother waving a wand and changing a pumpkin into a carriage, and Cinderella's rags into a beautiful ball gown is a transformation. But it was a change only in appearance – and it didn't last. Midnight came, and the coach became a pumpkin again, and Cinderella was once more dressed in rags. So we need to add to that definition a fourth element. Real transformation is something that lasts. We can use several words to describe that. "Continuity" is one. So is "sustainability," a term used more and more by church and service groups to talk about lasting effects for their acts of mercy.

---
[1] The Merriam-Webster Dictionary, Home of Office Edition. Springfield, Massachusetts: Merriam-Webster, Inc. p. 547

Given that definition, plus sustainability, as a working model, we will see, through this book, that Central Methodist has been transformed in structure and appearance. The changes have not transformed its character, but have led to a renewed understanding of, and commitment to, that character. This book will explore the process by which all that happened.

The transformations that we'll be studying did not happen overnight, nor were they the result of someone waving that magic wand. They took the combined efforts of many people – administration, staff, faculty, trustees, alumni, students. But they also needed the vision and energy of a leader. The New Deal, to cite a public example, did not happen without the labor of tens of thousands of people at all levels of American government and society. But they also did not happen without the vision and charismatic leadership of President Franklin Roosevelt. The same is true of Central. All the work of all those people was critical to the transformation of that "sleepy little college" into a bustling university. Also critical was the vision and leadership of President Marianne Inman. She did not have a magic wand, but she had something more important. She had a vision for the school that involved sharing leadership and commitment.

I agreed to write this book because Virginia Wood Bergsten asked me to. Jenny and I have been friends since our college days when we worked together on the Ragout. Out of that working relationship came a friendship and a deep respect for each other and each other's gifts. In the nearly 60 years since we graduated, we have continued that friendship and respect as we have worked, both together and in our own unique ways, to support the school we love. I am grateful to her for this opportunity.

This is not the first book about Central's history. In 1967 Dr. Frank Tucker, Class of 1917, published Central Methodist College, One Hundred and Ten Years. That volume covered the beginnings of the school, down to the middle 1960s. In 1986, Bartlett C. Jones published Central Methodist College, 1961-1986. This volume follows in their steps, taking the reader through a time of crisis in the history of the school, and then a period of transformation and growth that brings us to 2016 (when I closed the process) and the "sleepy little college" becoming a university.

A word about limitations. It is difficult to write about recent/ongoing history. Time has not yet worked its influence on the events we cover. We have not yet seen if the changes that are lifted up in these pages will be sustainable. That is one of the major challenges that are mentioned in the final chapter. I confess that the conclusions drawn in the book are largely my own, and I own the responsibility for them. A book written fifty years from now and covering the same time period as this own, will be able to see more clearly the results of the work that this book covers. Were the changes sustainable? What were the long-term results of the changes? But we do not live fifty years from now. We live in the present and this book is about the present and the near past. So we live with the limitations of incomplete understanding.

I am grateful to so many people who helped me understand the dynamics of the transformation at Central. At the top of the list is President Inman herself, who shared her thoughts and memories with me generously. Her spirit fills this book in many ways. The senior staff at Central shared time, insights, and resources with me freely. So did the faculty members and other staff whom I barraged with questions. Trustees opened doors to some of the steps that were required to transform the institution. President Roger Drake offered the resources of his office and of his own vision and commitment to Central.

If I were to name all of the individuals who have contributed to the understandings shared in this book, the introduction would be several more pages longer. I can only say "thank you" and hope that each of them knows, in his or her heart, how grateful I am for what they've shared with me. A special thanks goes to Dr. Jerry McClelland of the University of Minnesota, and to Virginia Bergsten, who read the entire manuscript and offered many helpful suggestions. The mistakes remain my own.

A special thanks to Delia Remington of Eagle Heights Press for her careful editorial work and business details.

Finally, I'm thankful for my wife, Beth, who shares my love for the school where we met. She has given freely of time for me to be gone doing research, for time fretting over not moving as quickly as I'd hoped, for time spent at my desk putting words on paper. She has supported me every step of the way, just as she has all through our life together. I owe her more than I can ever say.

John Gooch
Lees Summit, Mo.
October. 2017

TIMELINE

1972 Central Methodist College joins the allied health consortium and adds nursing program.

1977 Hall of Sponsors established

1980 Campus designated a National Historic District

1981 Philips Recreation Center opens

1982 Givens Hall becomes Central Methodist Alumni House

1983 Hairston Hall of Fame established.

1984 Besgrove-Hodge Sanctuary adds 86 acres to Central Methodist

1985 Hairston outdoor track and Calkins indoor track dedicated

1988 College Service Award and Young Alumni Award established

1989 2+2 program established with Mineral Area College

1993 Ashby-Hodge gallery established.

    2+2 Program with East Central College

1995 Marianne Inman becomes President of Central Methodist College

1996 Telecommunity Center opened. Master of Education first offered

2000 Alexander family provides a campus addition.

2001 First computer stations in the library

    Earl (1961) and Sunny Bates purchase and renovate Coleman Hall and make it available to CMU for formal functions.

2002 McMurry Hall renovated. Woodward and Burford Halls remodeled.

    Davis Field gets new bleachers

2003 Eyrie razed and construction on the new Student and Community Center begun.

    Denneny Career Center established

2004 Sesquicentennial celebration.

    Construction of the Student and Community Center.

    Central Methodist College becomes Central Methodist University

2006 Cindy Dudenhoffer appointed librarian

2007 Columbia campus opened in the Forum Boulevard Shopping Center. Information commons opens in Cupples Hall.

2007 – 2009 Athletic Facilities Renovation and Construction

2010 Central Methodist University -- St. Louis metropolitan area campus grand opening.

Regional campus in Macon with Moberly Area Community College on a 2+2 program

2011 Enrollment topped 3,000 for the first time. Fayette enrollment is 1,172, and CGES is 1,873

2012 Classic Hall Renovation complete

Center for Learning and Teaching Renovation

2013 Marianne Inman retires.

Roger Drake becomes President of Central Methodist University

2015 Thogmorton Center for Allied Health dedicated.

1

THE WORLD OF EDUCATION

The 1980s were not a good time for higher education, particularly for private liberal arts colleges. In early 1982, the United States suffered the worst recession (up to that time) since the Great Depression. There were 9 million persons unemployed in America. We discuss the implications of that for Central Methodist in more detail below. Hardly had the shock of that recession begun to subside when, on October 19, 1987, the stock market crashed. The Dow Jones Average suffered a 22.6% drop in one day. Financially, it was not a good time to have a child enter college!

In addition to the financial stress of those years, there were other factors that impacted higher education. They include: the end of the Vietnam War-era draft (which had an effect on enrollment, since many young men chose to attend school as a way of avoiding the draft); double-digit inflation; the variability in state and federal aid to private schools; the rise of community colleges; and the energy crisis.

All of these impacted (either directly or indirectly) enrollment in four-year private colleges. None of the results of the impacts was positive. The pool of prospective students dropped. Costs increased. Competition for the remaining pool of students grew because of community colleges, which were able to offer classes at a price well below what private colleges could offer. Internally, some schools suffered from a lack of competent financial management and could not make up the difference by increasing enrollment. Nationwide, over 100 institutions of higher learning either closed or merged. The closure rate of 2.9% for the decade of the 1980s was followed by a 3.3% closure rate for the 1990s. This latter probably represents schools whose viability was shocked by the events of the '80s, but managed to hang on into the 90s. In Missouri for example, Tarkio College closed its doors in 1992. The Assemblies of God Theological Seminary in Springfield merged with Central Bible College in 2013 to become Evangel, a school currently a part of the Heart of America Conference.[1]

The state of Missouri is perhaps over-served with higher education institutions. While Iowa, for example, has three state universities, strategically located in different parts of the state, Missouri has at least one public university in every section of the state. There are 13 four-year public universities, 23 two-year public colleges, 23 four-year independent colleges, and 2 two-year independent colleges. Given those numbers, it seems incredible that nearly 40% of college enrollment is in the independent college sector. And nearly 50% of all degrees are awarded by those colleges. At the graduate level, 60 percent of enrollment is at independent

---

[1] Data on school closings is taken from the Website *The Pietist Schoolman*, by Chris Gehrz.

universities and 70 percent of all degrees are awarded by them.[2] Given the reality of those numbers, it becomes obvious that Central Methodist (and other private colleges) provides a great educational service to the state at no cost to the taxpayer.

What are some of the implications of those numbers for Central Methodist University? Central's greatest competition for students is the public sector. The adoption of the A+ Schools program will probably mean that more high school graduates with a 3.0 GPA or higher will attend a community college or technical school rather than a four-year college. On the one hand, this is bad news for Central's enrollment, particularly on the Fayette campus. On the other hand, the 2 + 2 program offers a wide market for Central's relating to those community college graduates who want to work toward a four-year degree, either on the Fayette campus, or through the programs at our partner institutions. In 1997, when the strategic planning process was beginning to show action, the 2 + 2 program was about to "take off" and provide a new source of revenue for the college to expand its offerings, as well as take on deferred maintenance on the Fayette campus. (2+2 is "shorthand" for the programs that begin with 2 years in a community college, followed by 2 years in a four-year school to complete a bachelor's degree.)

Demographically, the context is not much brighter. The 1997-98 Self Study reported that, in Missouri, the number

---

[2] Inman, Marianne E. "Life-Span Learning – a Values-Driven System" in John Harrold and George Stuckey, Facilitating Authors, Learn or Die: 21st Century Community Learning. n.d., n.p. The 1998-1999 Self-Study Document said 35% and over 40% for the same categories. That is a change, but not a large one.

of high school graduates will increase less than 20%, from 56,000 in 1989-90 to just under 63,000 in 2008-09.[3] This means Central will be competing in a diminishing market, with 59 other schools seeking to enroll those same students.

At the same time, student expectations are higher than ever. Those expectations include a higher level of quality and service from what they would find in a public institution; attractive and up-to-date facilities; access to technology and to the Internet; and teaching/learning based on their preferred learning styles.[4]

The financial squeeze in which colleges find themselves stems from the fact that they have only two main sources of revenue. The first is student tuition and fees, along with room and board. The second is donor gifts and earnings from endowment. The latter is particularly hit hard in recessions/depressions, because giving by alumni and foundations is at least partially dependent on the stock market, and so is the earning ability of endowments. In contrast, public institutions (state universities, community colleges) also receive funds from the state budget, and local taxing districts (in the case of community colleges). That means they are able to offer lower tuition or, in the case of community colleges, significantly lower tuition. Private institutions, such as Central Methodist, have to discount tuition in order to compete in the same marketplace as public institutions.

What did that mean for Central Methodist? In 1982, the beginning of the great recession, the enrollment at Central was 569. There were several reasons for this. For Fiscal Year

---

3 "Central Methodist College, Strategic Planning for 2003, Draft #7," p. 2

4 *Ibid.*, p. 2-3

1982, the federal education money was not available until September. This was devastating for the college financially. As a part of dealing with the crisis, President Joe Howell initiated a reduction in faculty and staff.[5] The faculty-student ratio had declined to 9-1. The college had operating deficits every year from 1977-1982. The college was squeezed by inflation, which was rampant in the 1980s. Enrollments had declined. Student aid had increased dramatically. The plan to deal with this financial crisis involved cutting 22 non-faculty and 21 faculty. On November 12, the Curators approved the plan. The college declared a financial exigency. As one alumnus told me, "the first meeting of the Board I attended, they declared a financial exigency. I thought, what have I gotten myself into?" Declaring a financial exigency is one of the legal requirements before a school can dismiss tenured faculty. The day faculty and staff learned who would be let go (November 19, 1982), lives on in school history as "Black Friday." Alumni with whom I talked are sure that students first coined the name. In any event, it was a frightening time for the college.

The accredited status of the college was not damaged by this move. The savings projected by the plan were probably never realized in full. Overall, the plan probably saved the school in a time of crisis, but it did leave behind a welter of negative feelings. The exigency continued until the arrival of Dr. Marianne Inman as President, and even today there are references to Black Friday among faculty, trustees, and alumni.

---

[5] Material in this paragraph is taken primarily from Jones, Bartlett C., *Central Methodist College, 1961-1986.* n,p., 1986, pp. 181-187

In a related side issue, Glenn Cox, recently retired chair of the Board of Trustees, and a Curator (as they were known then) recalls an off-the-record meeting of 8-10 members of the board to discuss Central merging with another school, because of the financial situation. This meeting took place during the 1986-88 period. There was no specific school named as a possible merger, just a general exploration of the idea. The suggestion didn't go anywhere, but the mere fact of discussing it indicates some of the fear that the college would not be able to continue as a viable institution if it stood alone.

Fortunately, enrollment increased to 613 in 1983 and, in 1990, to 767. In 1994, it had risen to 857.[6] There continued, however, to be financial problems, since the growth in students did not match the growth in costs. By 1995, there was a cumulative debt of over $1,000,000, much of that to food services. The debt, as debt always does, meant years of deferred maintenance, lack of capability to improve technology and other innovations, inability to increase faculty salaries, and other problems which we will address in later chapters.

During this period of the 1980s, there were also some developments that boded well for the future. One was the beginnings of the relationships with community colleges. The first step was taken in the relationship with Mineral Area Community College. The program with Mineral Area Community College, as it was set up, was the perfect marriage of 2 and 4 year programs. Persons living in the Mineral Area who had completed two years, could finish their baccalaureate degree without having to move out of the area. That meant they did not have to uproot families, leave jobs,

---
6 Enrollment figures taken from *CMU Factbook, 2015 – 2016*.

and so on, but could finish their education "long-distance." Mineral Area College was asked to provide one furnished office, up to five furnished classrooms, and one computer lab. Central Methodist took on the rest. Up to five separate classes were offered each eight-week term. This was the first of many such relationships with Central Methodist, the full story of which is told in Chapter 8. Initially, there was not a great boost to Central's finances, but over the years there have been millions of dollars from the partnerships.

The second partnership, with East Central College in Union, came in 1993. Again, it was the opportunity for area residents to earn a bachelor's degree without having to leave their home community that made the partnership a natural match.

Another step into the future came with the establishment of the I-TV program. This form of video-conferencing, new then, is now available practically everywhere in the state. Central was the one higher education partner in a consortium with five rural school districts – Slater, Glasgow, New Franklin, Pilot Grove, and Bunceton. The program offered instruction to high schools through interactive television. Most of the courses were offered for dual credit. The system uses split screen technology, with the capacity to reach four different locations (including the site at Central where the teacher is located). Over the years, Central's participation has grown so that we have been the number one user of interactive television service.

Two years after the beginnings of I-TV (1993) Central Methodist became one of four sites for the establishment of a TeleCommunity Center, thanks to Southwestern Bell. (The other locations were University of Missouri, St. Louis,

Kansas City Metropolitan College – Science and Technology Center, and Three Rivers Community College at Poplar Bluff.) These centers provided computer instruction, individual computer stations, and videoconferencing capability. Most of the learners were area adults, many of them senior citizens. These centers were phased out by 2000, because of the growth in personal computers. For the few years it was in existence, however, it was a boon to the Fayette area and to adult learning.

In 1995, the Missouri Interactive Telecommunications Education Network (known as MIT-E) came into being. This made possible the development of dual credit programs in high schools. The first dual credit program was with the Chillicothe, Mo. school district. Central Methodist provides dual credit courses through interactive television. The University can teach interactive courses to any school district in Missouri with ITV that wants it. Today, the program has grown from one high school to one hundred.

A third step toward the future for Central Methodist was the nursing program. Actually begun in 1974, under the leadership of Dr. John Smart, as an associate degree program, the full degree program started in the 1980s. Today, the nursing program includes a Masters program, with degrees in clinical nurse leadership and nursing education.

Another sign of hope for the future was the development of the Hall of Sponsors scholarship program, designed to help individuals and churches to sponsor scholarships for individual students. Today, there are 257 Hall of Sponsors scholarships and counting. Local United Methodist churches were invited to contribute the funds for a scholarship, and many responded enthusiastically. Alumni were also committed donors to the Hall of Sponsors. The Class of 1959 has donated 17, and counting, but other alumni have also given generously.

As historian Thomas Lindsay says, in another context, "the first (step) is valuable not for what it is in itself, but for what it represents and for what comes after it."[7] The beginnings we have discovered in this chapter were valuable for themselves, but even more valuable for that into which they grew. As President Howell prepared to retire, he had steered Central Methodist through some rough times, especially financially, and laid the groundwork for what would become the explosion of growth and change in the immediate future.

---

7 Lindsay, Thomas M., *A History of the Reformation. Volume I: The Reformation in Germany from Its Beginning to the Religious Peace of Augsburg.* New York: Charles Scribner's Sons, 1926, p. 399

2
A New Day Dawns

The year 1995 was a critical one for Central Methodist. Dr. Joe Howell had retired after 18 years as president. He left behind a legacy that included growth and some hopeful signs for the future. His legacy, however, also included major debt, years of deferred maintenance, and other areas of concern.

Dr. Howell had set his retirement to give a 5-year period for the transition and selection process. A transition committee, appointed by the Board, met with a previous search committee and read several books on searching for a president. This study led to a focus on some key issues. One of the keys was a focus on fiscal responsibility because of the financial situation in which the school found itself. A second was a strong academic background. A third was a dynamic leadership style, one that could inspire others. And, finally they were looking for someone who knew where the field of higher education was heading.

There was a felt need to work with a professional search firm in order to give the Board a wider, more national potential pool of candidates. So the committee provided the above criteria to the search firm as a place to begin. The professional team took the criteria and placed an announcement in the *Chronicle of Higher Education*.

At the first meeting of the search committee dealing with selection, there were approximately 100 resumes to be read and categorized. Several meetings later, the number was reduced to the actual number of members of the search committee. The task then was for each member of the search committee to contact one candidate and determine 1) why that person wanted to be President of Central, and 2) if that person had the credentials for the position.

Finally, three persons were chosen to invite to campus for interviews. Even at this point, Marianne Inman was the leading candidate.

In terms of fiscal responsibility, the committee probed the candidates extensively. Dr. Marianne Inman spoke well to the issue of financial responsibility and a balanced budget.

As we will see in Chapter four, she was able to make significant changes quickly in the financial picture at Central, and to work from a balanced budget within her first year.

Dr. Inman had a strong academic background. She has a Ph.D. in languages and had served, among other posts, on the President's Commission on Foreign Language and International Studies. She came to the vetting process from Northland College, in Ashland, Wisconsin. Northland is a very small school, with a distinctive program in environmental education. Dr. Inman was able to speak powerfully to the value of distinctive programs. She also did not say that she would institute a program of environmental education at Central. Rather, she knew Central's strengths and had ideas for how to build on those strengths. When we talk about curriculum in Chapter Seven, we'll see what she considered distinctive about Central's offerings, and how the school could build on those strengths in several ways.

As we saw in Chapter 1, Missouri is over-populated with institutions of higher education. Missouri has the University system of three major schools, plus other public universities in every corner of the state. It is hard for small private colleges to compete in that market. Central is a small college in a rural community, with students coming primarily from Missouri. Student recruiting and retention is a continual struggle competing against so many state schools. Dr. Inman had a good strategic view of the situation and how Central could operate in it.

Another plus for her was her United Methodist roots. Central began with a statement by its founders that it would be the only Methodist college in Missouri. An awareness of the United Methodist heritage would be a plus for any candidate for the presidency, even though there was no longer a need for the president to be Methodist clergy.

At the conclusion of the three visits, there was no hesitation on the part of the committee that Dr. Inman was the right person for the job. They wanted her to become President. She wanted to be President! It was a perfect match – the right person in the right place at the right time.

One comment from a member of the search committee bears repeating. He said it helps to be lucky, or in theological terms, "blessed." There is always a better than 50/50 chance that you'll get the wrong person. It was a blessing, indeed, for

Central that the search committee beat the odds and got the right person.[1]

So the committee recommended that Dr. Inman be chosen as the new President of Central Methodist College (as it was then). The Board received that recommendation and voted in favor.

What Next?

There is a classic scene in Lewis Carroll's Alice in Wonderland, where Alice asks the Cheshire Cat for directions.

> "Would you tell me, please, which way I ought to go from here?"
>
> "That depends a good deal on where you want to get to," said the Cat.
>
> "I don't much care where ---" said Alice.
>
> "Then it doesn't matter which way you go," said the Cat.
>
> "--- so long as I get somewhere," Alice added as an explanation.
>
> Oh, you're sure to do that," said the Cat, "if you only walk long enough."[2]

That "conversation" typifies the task before an incoming executive. There are all sorts of things calling for her attention. Which to do first? For President Inman, the most important task of all was a revision of the mission of the university. Fighting the fires of specific problems could be done while that basic task was being completed, but moving forward was more than just trying to get 'somewhere.' Where did Central Methodist want to go? That was the key question.

---

[1] The material about the search, as well as this comment, comes from Jay Jacobs, in a telephone interview, Spring 2017. Jay was a part of the search committee.

[2] Carroll, Lewis, *The Annotated Alice: The Definitive Edition*. W.W. Norton and Co., 1999. p. 96

The result of serious study, thought, receiving input from faculty, staff, students, alumni, was the new mission statement:

> "Central Methodist University prepares students to make a difference in the world by emphasizing academic and professional excellence, ethical leadership, and social responsibility."

The college (as it was then) also listed values by which the mission could be enriched and lived out. Those values included:[3]

> Our Wesleyan heritage and unique place as the only United Methodist-related university in Missouri.
> The location of the main campus as an opportunity for students to live and learn in a safe setting.
> A strong liberal arts education.
> A university life that emphasizes honesty, integrity, civility, and a strong sense of personal responsibility as integral elements of character and leadership.
> A spirit of community and caring.

As the book progresses, we'll look in more detail at these values and how they are lived out. But note here that the focus is on "seeking knowledge, truth, and wisdom, valuing freedom, honesty, civility and diversity, and living lives of service and leadership."

Further, the educational goals contained in the core documents state that "the Central Methodist University experience engenders...student growth in knowledge, personal integrity, spirituality, and professional competence.

---

[3] The material on values and goals is all taken directly from the Central Methodist University Core Documents.

In addition students are challenged to develop a sense of global citizenship and a commitment to the betterment of the world." That statement mandates that education is more than "information passing from the notes of the professor to the notes of the student without passing through the head of either." The core document recognizes and reflects that reality. It states that students with a CMU education are prepared to:

Academically

- Demonstrate knowledge of the liberal arts and academic specialties as well as technical skills and professional competencies.
- Think critically and conceptually and apply their knowledge and skills to the solving of problems.
- Communicate accurately and effectively through listening, speaking, and writing.

Character

- Continue to develop self-knowledge, confidence, and a sense of honor and commitment by assuming responsibility and leadership in the service of others.
- Seek an understanding of ideas, issues, and events within and beyond their immediate community and appreciate the gifts of diversity.
- Evaluate their personal strengths and abilities, and explore appropriate career choices in a changing world.
- Have the courage to make decisions based on considerations of ethical, aesthetic, economic, and environmental consequences.
- Commit themselves to a life exemplifying values in relationships with self, family, church, university, and community.

Those are incredibly important life goals. On a personal note, I have spent over 50 years working with youth and am keenly aware of how their development needs to be pointed in the directions suggested by these goals, particularly those listed under character. The leadership at Central Methodist University did not arrive at all these statements overnight. They were developed over a period of months and years as the sense of direction for the University was clarified in the minds of senior leadership and affirmed by faculty, students, and alumni.

So. There is a road map. The new mission statement and related documents spell out what Central is about and the goals for student development. People have bought into the destination and the direction that needs to be taken in order to reach that destination. What comes next?

In 1997, the College asked four architectural firms to present proposals for a campus facilities master plan. One of those firms was selected to do the master planning process. In addition, a Strategic Planning Team was selected from college constituencies to develop action plans in the areas of: enrollment, academic and student life, campus facilities and equipment, human resources, and resource generation.[4]

One step was to focus on the quality of the living environments. President Inman remembers thinking, as she toured the dormitories after her arrival, "If I had a child ready for college, I wouldn't want him living here." Remember that the financial struggles of the late 80s and early 90s led to years of deferred maintenance, and by 1995 buildings fell

---
4 *Central Methodist: A Character-Building College.* Self-Study Report, 1997-1998. p. 5

below the standards that students and their families expected. Residence halls lacked basic comforts and efficiencies. Classrooms and laboratories were outdated. The student union had been a temporary building moved from Camp Crowder in Neosho in 1947. Athletic facilities ranked near the bottom of the conference. There was an immediate need to upgrade facilities all over the campus – even as other crises begged for attention. Plus, the students of the 90s wanted more amenities. Part of that generation graduated from suburban high schools with buildings less than 5-10 years old, up-to-date labs, modern classrooms. Others in that generation graduated from older, smaller, high schools but schools that had tried to keep up with the times. Almost all of that generation was accustomed to air-conditioning at home, probably at school, and in other buildings in their communities. They were not satisfied with the comfort level of dormitories and classrooms without air-conditioning. This made recruitment harder, and student admissions and retention suffered. That led to new problems financially, as there was less income than needed from tuition and student fees.

The material in the previous paragraphs begins to sound like the labors of Hercules. In a later chapter, we will deal with the issue of living and study environments in some detail, but they are mentioned here to show that the lofty statements in official documents then needed to be turned into realities on the ground. That they did become realities shows the commitment to change and progress on the part of Central's leadership team.

In her address at the opening convocation in the fall of 1995, the new president, Dr. Marianne Inman, spelled out for students and faculty what she considered to be crucial for the ongoing life of Central.⁵

She referenced the United Methodist Church's belief in social justice and in the ability and responsibility of each of us to make a positive difference in the world. Then she said "Central Methodist College carries on that tradition of standing up for what is right and for what we know and believe to be true." She went on to say that Central does not just prepare students for jobs, but teaches values and principles of life. After discussing some of the evidence that lying and cheating are not only pervasive in American life, but also thought to be OK, she cited the Rutgers Center for Academic Integrity which some have suggested indicates "yearning for a higher order of things and behavior on a more elevated moral level."

President Inman then pointed out that Central Methodist stands for something and began to describe what that something is. First, for her, were honesty and integrity. These are qualities that come from deep within us, and need constant practice and reinforcement. Another core quality or value, she said, is love. We all need to love and to be able to love. We also have a deep need to be loved. To love others, it is necessary to love oneself. This means to recognize that you are a person of worth and dignity. It means valuing and honoring yourself. It means risking, being unafraid of making mistakes. Loving oneself – and others – means caring for the physical bodies

---

5 The following summary is taken from Marianne Inman, "What Will You Stand For?" in *Presidential Papers*, Volume 13, No. 2, September 1997. The Division of Higher Education, General Board of Higher Education and Ministry, the United Methodist Church.

we live in. It means respecting others, and treating them with civility.

Another fundamental value for Central is the emphasis on excellence and the expectation of high standards. Doing something "good enough" or "just enough to get by" is a disservice to everyone.

All these core values – honesty, integrity, love, respect, civility, excellence, and high standards – have to do with our ability and our obligation to make a positive difference in the world. In a closing paragraph, Dr. Inman challenged her listeners to think about how they will make a difference in the world, and asked them, "what will you stand for?"

Even after only a few months as President, Dr. Inman was clear about the values that mattered to her, and that clarity would guide her work and leadership at Central Methodist. A new day was dawning.

3

TRANSFORMING THE BOARD OF CURATORS

A significant transformation in the life of Central Methodist during this crucial period was in the governing board. From its inception, Central was legally governed by a Board of Curators. According to the by-laws, the Curators might be composed of no fewer than ten members and no more than thirty. Eighteen of the thirty were to be appointed by the two Annual Conferences of the United Methodist Church of Missouri. Three (the President of the College, the Bishop of the Missouri Area of the United Methodist Church, and the President of the National Alumni Association of the college) were *ex officio*. Nine members might be elected "at large". Of the twenty-seven elected members, at least eight had to be alumni of Central Methodist: at least one half must be members of the United Methodist Church; and at least one-third had to be residents of the State of Missouri.[1] In fact, as someone allegedly said, the typical

---

1 Self-Study, 1997-1998, p. 11-12

board member was a United Methodist alumnus of the college, living anywhere in the State of Missouri. In reality, the board often did not have thirty members, as one of the annual conferences did not always appoint its nine allotted members every year.

By 2008, the by-laws had been changed to enlarge the number to 40 Trustees. The change in both the name and the number is significant. As someone quipped, a curator is someone who watches over a museum collection. Important as that role might be, the implication is that he/she is focused on the past or present, not the future. One could say, in contrast, that a trustee is someone who is aware of the responsibility of making what exists even better. One suspects that the name change had a subtle, but unmistakable, effect on the way the board members approached their duties. Certainly the board during the first two decades of the new century took their responsibility for the future of the college very seriously, indeed.

The number is also significant. The larger board of trustees included a broader diversity of age, gender, ethnicity, expertise, denominational affiliation, and non-alumni persons. The change in number happened gradually, first to 33 members, then to 36, and presently to 40. There are, at present, no plans to continue enlarging the trustees.

Another transformation was the addition of women to the Board. Central College's first century was governed by an exclusively male Board of Curators. Given the legal status of women in the United States during that century, and the status of women within the Methodist Church and its predecessor bodies, that is not surprising. However, women were voting in public elections, seated at the General

Conferences of the church, and otherwise making their presence felt long before they were invited to become members of the Board of Curators of Central Methodist.

One hundred years after the founding of the college, during the year of Brown vs. Board of Education (1954), Central elected the first woman to the Board. The material on women members of the Board was written by Trustee Emerita Virginia Bergsten. Martha Smith Luck – a 1931 Central graduate with a B.A. in English, a master's degree from Northwestern University, and the Dean of the Evening School at Northwestern – became that first. During her tenure on the Board, she served as Secretary and as a Member of the Executive Committee. In conversation with Florence Gaddis, wife of Central's renowned history professor, Dr. M. E. Gaddis, one alum recalls her comment regarding the Luck appointment: "Finally the Board has chosen a female and one whose experience and expertise are in higher education."

During the 35 years between 1954 and 1989, only six other females became members of the Board. One was chosen from the Missouri Methodist community; two were sisters; one was a William Jewell graduate; and one was the daughter of the Chairman of the Board.

During the early 1990s, there was a short period when only one female board member regularly attended the full meetings and summer retreats. Two others were able to attend only sporadically because of professional commitments and health demands. Feeling singular among the 27 male members led to her passion for continual lobbying to close the gender gap. As the college student body has been consistently 49/51male/female, or vice versa, this one female

Board member could not realistically nor reliably represent half of the enrolled undergraduate community.

Almost a century and a half after Central College was founded, the Board of Curators chose Marianne Inman as the first woman President of the College. At about the same time, Ann Sherer was elected as Bishop of the United Methodist Church and appointed to Missouri – our first female Bishop. By virtue of their professional positions, these two path-breaking women served as ex officio members of the CMC Board. At the 2000 summer Board retreat, the female count around the conference table totaled seven, led by the leadership and inspiration of the Bishop and Central's first female CEO. The maximum number for a full Board, at that time, was 30.

As female membership has continually increased, women have been drawn from varied professional and volunteer roles. There have been Methodist pastors, elementary, secondary, and college teachers, art curators, a writer, and highly responsible business leaders from companies such as IBM. One long-serving trustee and alumna was a prominent civic and philanthropic stalwart from St. Louis. Another alumna is the Vice-President of a small town bank. A former secretary of the Board led a Northeastern suburban community through the transition of its local high school to its establishment as one of the leading academic high schools in the United States. Clearly, the addition of women to the Board has been transformative.

Currently, forty individuals can be elected to the Board of Trustees (the transition from the term "Curator" to "Trustee" occurred August 4, 2005). Of the current forty trustees during the 2016-2017 academic year, nine are female, almost one-fourth of the full Board. Five of the current female members have had positions in businesses dealing with accounting, financial management, and technology. From the field of medicine, the CMU Board (CMC became CMU in May, 2004) boasts an oncologist and an anesthesiologist. The oncologist serves as the current Vice Chair and is slated to become the first female Chair of the Board. Two other members are from the field of education; and of the eight standing committee chairs, three are women. One third of the Executive Committee is female.

At the 2016 Board Retreat, a humorous moment occurred as a reminder of the change in female membership. During the morning break, there was a line waiting to use the women's restroom, a sea change from the time of one female trustee.

Plaudits to the CMU Board of Trustees for their significant progress in number and quality of female trustees and their commitment to the University's vision. How significant this representation and example of leadership must be for the university's female undergraduate and graduate students.

Certainly, more growth in female representation will occur, but now is the time for devoted attention to greater Board representation from the minority community and the alumni of CMU's extended studies locations. Another 100 years must not elapse before the CMU Board becomes fully representative of all its students.

Much of the work of the Board is done in committees. There are eight standing committees: Advancement and Alumni Relations; Buildings and Grounds; Graduate and Extended Studies; Finance; Learning and Teaching; Strategic Directions; Student Development; and Trusteeship and Governance. In addition, there is an Executive Committee, consisting of the officers of the Board, the Chairs of the Standing Committees, and the President. One day of the Board meeting is spent in committees, and one day in plenary session. The current officers of the Board (at the time of this writing) are Robert "Tad" Perry, Chair; Nancy Peacock, Vice-Chair; and Bruce Addison, Secretary.

4

Transforming Finances

The year 1995 was a crucial one for the financial life of Central Methodist. As the chart below shows, the previous five years had been ones of deficit spending, where expenses exceeded revenues.

90/91-$602,985
91/92-$186,474
92/93-$112,450
93/94-$ 68,681
94/95-$ 54,356
95/96+$ 75,433[1]

Note that even though the deficit was getting smaller each year, the debt was still piling up.

In 1995, the accounts payable were $1.3 million. In the fall of 1997, accounts payable were down to less than $300,000.[2] How did that happen?

---

1 *Overview of Central Methodist College*, 1999, p, 11
2 Self-Study, 1998-1999, p. 152

A major reason for the deficits (other than spending more money than the school had) was the competition for students presented by the rise of community colleges. They came into being in the late 60s and early 70s, and presented more choices for higher education. In addition, their tuition is "next to nothing" and students took advantage of these opportunities. Student enrollment at Central declined, with the attendant drop in income. President Howell's move to the 2 + 2 program with the community colleges would make a huge difference to Central, but by 1990 that was not paying off yet. In addition, church support was down. The Missouri Conferences of The United Methodist Church voted to change monies given to Central from an apportionment to an asking. The former term meant an amount designated for each church to pay toward support of Central. The latter meant churches could choose what amount they wanted to give. Some congregations continued to give generously, but overall, the amount of financial support went down at a time when it was most needed.

There were several serious consequences as a result of that. One was deferred maintenance. For the years 90/91 through 94/95, there were no funds in the operating budget for maintenance. It is commonly understood that putting off maintenance on buildings does not save money in the long run, but costs more. Anyone who has ever had to delay replacing a damaged roof knows what that means. However, it is also well-known that one can't make repairs on a building if one does not have the money! A second consequence was a federal requirement in 1994 that Central provide a letter of credit in order for students to continue to be eligible to receive federal financial aid. This was not a simple task.

Trustee Lou Bailey said that the Trustees were, almost literally, "on their knees" with banks trying to get such a letter. Finally, Mercantile Bank in St. Louis came through with the letter. Without it, and without the federal financial aid, many students would have not been able to continue at Central, which would have made the financial situation of the school even worse. A third consequence was that Central's debt was mounting up. In 1995, that debt was, as we have seen, over $1,000,000, most of it owed to food services.

So, how did the school get out of that debt? Not the net gain from the relationships with community colleges. In 94-95, that net was only $150,000. The key was President Inman's insistence on a change in the business model to zero-based budgeting. Everything was on the table, every year, so that there would be a balanced budget. The line of credit paid off the debt, and the budget included money to pay back the line of credit. Julee Sherman, Vice-President for Finance and Administration, says that they had been delaying paying bills as long as possible, up to 45 days. In the new model, they paid all bills every other week.[3] Every year since 95/96, there has been a balanced budget and a surplus of revenue over expenses.

The visit to the campus in March of 1998 by the North Central Association of Colleges and Schools reported significant progress on the financial front. "The close control and monitoring of the College's finances in the last three years have created a much stronger fiscal posture of Central Methodist College. A surplus is projected for FY 97-8 and budgeted for FY99; and since FY96 each year's operating budget at the time of preparation has included a $200,000

---
[3] Interview with Julee Sherman

reserve. The Team was impressed with the progress made to date and understands that the President and the Board of Curators are committed to continued enhancement of the fiscal condition of the College."[4] In addition, in fiscal years 1996, 1997, and 1998 the budget included a salary raise pool that exceeded the rate of inflation.[5]

That same report indicated that the College had made some progress with deferred maintenance, and indicated that a major funding campaign would be needed because deferred maintenance "is evident in most buildings on campus."[6]

As of June 30, 1999 (the close of the fiscal year), there were still outstanding notes payable, most of them for upgrades to buildings (part of that deferred maintenance), but they were all being paid on time.

Another giant step forward was the most successful capital campaign in the history of the institution (up to that time). This was the $30 million dollar Campaign for Central. As we have noted in other places, the condition of many of the buildings on campus was sub-par. The prime example, though not the only one, was the Eyrie. The student union had been a Quonset hut officer's club at Camp Crowder in southwest Missouri that was moved to the campus in 1947 as a "temporary solution" to the lack of such a union. Several attempts had been made in the 1980s and 1990s to build a replacement, but the funds were never raised. The inability to raise the funds contributed to a sense of futility

---

[4] "Report of a Visit to Central Methodist College, March 2-4, 1998, Fayette Missouri for the Commission on Institutions of Higher Education of the North Central Association of Colleges and Schools," p. 7

[5] Self-Study, p. 154

[6] Ibid.

and discouragement about ever breaking out of that rut. In addition, both the residence halls and the classrooms were outdated. In spite of considerable skepticism about the size of the campaign, it was a great success, raising over $34 million. Glenn Cox (Trustee Chair) says he thinks the campaign was the pivot on which Central turned. Or, as President Inman said, it moved us from "do you think it will happen this time" to "what comes next?" It was followed by a $5 million campaign for Central Athletics, which improved all the athletic facilities. A major bond issue in 2001 raised money for renovating McMurry and Howard-Payne residence halls, and the $5.5 million campaign "A Classic Renaissance" for the renovation and conversion of Classic Hall was also a great success. Details on the buildings will be found in a later chapter.

It is important to note here the interconnection of what happens on a college campus. The capital campaigns brought in large sums of money. That money provided improvements that made the campus more attractive to both current and prospective students. Alumni seeing the improvements and the new spirit increased their giving. The result was more income for the school, which made possible things such as faculty salary increases, and more upgrades to buildings. Just as a downward spiral can feed upon itself, so an upward spiral also feeds upon itself. Success can, indeed, breed success.

In addition to building improvement, the endowment fund also gained from the campaigns and other alumni gifts. Assets in the endowment grew from $8,100,000 in 1991 to $16,408,728 in 1999 – more than double. The endowment has continued to grow and as of 2015 it stands at $36.34 million.

5

Transforming the Campus

Physically, Central is an "old" campus. Brannock Hall goes back to the founding of the school in 1854 – or perhaps earlier than that, to Howard High School. So it comes as no surprise to learn that, in 1980, some 12 campus buildings were placed on the National Register of Historic Places. On the one hand, it's exciting that the campus is so honored. On the other, that means a lot of buildings are old and need expensive repair and upkeep. The definition of transformation this book uses for a working model calls for a change in structure, appearance, or character that is sustainable. The physical transformation on the campus will show all of those changes, though the character of the campus still remains.

The Dark Years

In the "dark years," when Central was struggling financially, there was still some movement toward campus improvements. In 1981, the Perry Philips Recreation Center (with the E. E. Rich Memorial Pool) opened on what was previously the practice field for the marching band, among other uses. In 2014, the building name became Philips-Robb to include the late Mark Robb, who spent 37 years at CMU and passed away in 2013. A $1 million renovation and expansion was completed in 2014.

In 1984, the Besgrove-Hodge Sanctuary added 86 acres to the campus. That Sanctuary is used for academic purposes such as biology research, Earth Day activities for area schools and, most recently, the Criminal Justice program's forensic research. In the latter case, road kills, spent shells, and other items are buried in the fall and then, in the spring, students come out to search for them and answer questions about them. The sanctuary is also used for ropes courses. The Kountz family donated land that is currently slated for development at a later time. The University has the use of the land north of the football field (now the practice field) from a gift to the Howard County Foundation through Fred and Barbara Alexander. In 1985, the Hairston outdoor track and the Calkin indoor track were dedicated. They made a significant improvement to a part of the athletic facilities. And, in 1993, the Ashby-Hodge gallery of American Art was established.

The Ashby-Hodge Gallery of American Art

Dr. Lawrence Ashby was a dentist in Pekin, Illinois, who had been a student at Central in the 1940s. He started buying art in the 1960s, focusing on Thomas Hart Benton and his students. He expressed an interest in giving part of his art to Central, but didn't like the Stephens Museum as a location. President Howell guaranteed space in Cupples Hall for the art. Robert and Anna Mae Hodge who were also students in the 1940s and were influential in the building of the North Kansas City Hospital put up the money to change the bookstore space in Cupples Hall to an art gallery. Dr. Ashby and his wife Loretta donated his paintings a few at a time until his death, when the collection came to Central. The school received about 150 paintings in total.

Tom Yancey (1954) was the first curator of the collection, and Dr. Joseph Geist was active in the collecting and display of the art.

President Howell promised to buy the Robert Graham Missouri Historical Heritage paintings. When he retired, that purchase was in limbo, partly because there were no funds to pay for them. President Inman was considering withdrawing the offer when Dr. Geist took her to meet Mr. Graham. Dr. Geist says that President Inman and Mr. Graham spoke Czech to each other and that he is convinced that's why the university owns those paintings today. Most of them are currently on display in the Student and Community Center.

Soon Yancey and Geist were doing shows of the art, which were well attended by the community, by alumni, and by art fanciers from across the state. But the space on the lower level of Cupples Hall was not really adequate for an art gallery. When Classic Hall was being re-done (see below), President Inman asked Dr. Geist if he wanted to move the gallery there. Geist said yes, not really knowing to what he was saying yes. Today, the space in Classic is almost double that in Cupples. The University continues to get collections because the gallery has an excellent reputation. Paintings are hung all over the campus and still there is a lack of storage space, but that is a nice problem to have. In addition, the gallery has become known across the state and beyond for the quality of its collection.

Dormitories Remodeled and Renovated

In 2002, McMurry Hall, a long-time residence for men, was closed, gutted, and remodeled into suites as a co-ed dorm. The work was made possible because of a bond issue by the college, the first of its kind. Past Trustee President Glenn Cox said that the bond issue was a leap of faith by the Trustees, and not everyone was certain it was a good idea. Could the college financially afford such a project? As it turned out, the bonds sold well, and the college was able to begin repaying them so well that an additional $2 million was added. McMurry Hall today is a different world from the one that generations of students remember. The central lounge is a showplace. The suites are more congenial to today's students than the old double rooms with a communal bathroom/shower room down the hall.

At the same time, Burford Hall and Woodward Hall, also residences for men, were remodeled and updated. Burford had been a state of the art dormitory when it was completed in 1960, but forty years later, it was definitely in need of work. The same was true of Woodward. Today, they are again top of the line residence halls. In addition, most of the residence halls now have air-conditioning.

Davis Field also got new bleachers. Other building renovation and upgrades include: infrastructure upgrades to T. Berry Smith Hall, air-conditioning for Puckett Field House, room upgrades for Holt Hall and Howard Payne, elevator installation in Howard-Payne, wireless installation across the campus, renovation of the conservatory, air-conditioning for

Holt Hall, a new softball field locker room building, and land acquisitions in properties adjoining the campus.

The Eyrie Is Gone

The iconic photograph of all the new things happening on campus is President Inman swinging a sledge hammer against a brick wall on the outside of the old Eyrie. One doubts that the blow did much except raise some dust, but it was an exciting moment nonetheless. The old Eyrie was being razed to make room for the new Student and Community Center. We all know the story of the Eyrie. It had been a Quonset hut officers' club building at Camp Crowder in southwest Missouri during World War II. In 1947, it was moved to the Central campus as a "temporary" student union. For years, it continued to be a gathering place and social center for the life of the college. A large addition was built onto it in 1965 to provide more space for dances and other activities, but, by 2003, it had long outlived its usefulness. Several attempts had been made to raise the funds to replace it, but they had all failed. These failed attempts had added to the discouragement about the campus around the close of the millennium.

The Campaign for Central, which we have seen earlier was described by both Trustee President Cox and College President Inman as the pivot point, raised $34.5 million toward a $30 million goal (that many had considered far too ambitious). Some $2.5 million of that had come from matching gifts from the Mabee and Kresge Foundations.

Work on the new Student and Community Center drew alumni attention immediately, and many of them made semi-regular trips to the campus just to check on progress.

The third floor of the building, comprising the Bergsten Dining Hall, opens onto the campus quadrangle. This floor also houses the Eyrie Café, the name being all that remains from the original building. The fourth floor houses conference rooms. Going down the hill, the second floor houses offices, the campus bookstore, mail room, and activity rooms. The first floor houses the Living History display, offices, weight rooms, the athletic training department, and connects to Puckett Field House. It opens on to a large parking lot.

The building was a showpiece at the Sesquicentennial celebration at Homecoming of 2004 and is used by both campus and community organizations for meetings. When President Inman retired, at the retirement/farewell dinner, Trustee President Cox announced that the trustees had voted to name the building the Inman Student and Community Center, and that the additional name for the building had been put in place while a large crowd was enjoying dinner in Puckett Field House.

Classic Hall

Once the home of classes for hundreds of students, Classic had been closed since 1980 because of its deteriorating condition, the anticipated cost of repairs, the cost of energy to heat and cool it, and because the low enrollment at the time did not warrant keeping it operational.

Classic had been built in 1911 as an academic building for Howard-Payne College. It originally held classrooms, faculty offices, theatre, and even a gymnasium. When Howard-Payne became part of Central College in the early 1920s, it became the home of classics – English, foreign languages, philosophy and religion, history, and other disciplines. Several times it was reworked, including building a giant concrete stairway in the middle of the building, and putting glass blocks in the windows.

But for 31 years it sat there, home only of pigeons and the occasional intruding graffiti artist. No one seemed to know quite what to do with it. One thought, always, was simply to raze it. But the asbestos in the building put a damper on that idea, as it did on several others. An alumni couple in Fayette considered buying it and turning it into an inn. Again, cost made that idea impractical. Another suggestion was to remodel it and move the library from Cupples Hall, making it a library for both the campus and the Fayette community. None of the suggestions gained much headway. Then in 2008, Mr. Tom Celli, of an architectural firm in Pittsburgh, PA, did a "walkabout" of the campus and asked if anyone had ever thought of making it a center for music and the arts? This suggestion came at a time when the band and choir both had outgrown their space and needed room in which to grow.

In the fall of 2008, the Trustees approved a fundraising campaign to renovate Classic Hall. The campaign was known as "A Classic Renaissance...The Next 100 Years." Money came in, and the Mabee Foundation gave Central a challenge grant of $1,080,500, provided the school raised the remainder of the funds by the fall of 2011 – a sum of over $1.3 million. The challenge was met!

As work began on Classic Hall, an object that looked like an oil well pump was seen working in front of the building. An alumnus wanted to know if we had struck oil on the campus (probably tongue-in-cheek). The answer was "no," that was drilling to provide geothermal energy for heating and cooling the building. Another first for Central!

The dedication of the restored building took place at Homecoming 2012. It now houses the Ashby-Hodge Gallery of American Art on the first floor, and the rest of the building is given over to the Swinney Conservatory. Offices, the music library, and practice rooms occupy the second floor and rehearsal spaces for the bands and choirs are on the third floor.

At the dedication, alumni were overheard looking at the new spaces and trying to remember what classes were held in the space when they were in school. That turned out to be the game of the week!

The Thogmorton Center for Allied Health

The Campaign for the Heart of Central set a goal of $20 million. Of that, $6,500,000 was for the new James and Helen Thogmorton Center for Allied Health. The newest building on the Central campus, it provides lab space of athletic training, occupational and physical therapy. There are expanded, high-tech simulation labs for nursing (that look exactly like modern hospital rooms), and added classroom space for allied health programs. The building was needed because space limitations imposed by nursing accreditation meant Central could not enroll all the qualified applicants for the program. A serious need was not being met.

To help meet those needs, Jay Jacobs, a Fayette native who works in the world of finance in California, and his wife Kelly donated $3.6 million for the center. Jay was asked if he wanted naming rights for the building. He said no, but called back in a couple of weeks and asked if the naming rights were still available. Told that they were, he said he wanted to name the new building for "Dean T" and Helen Thogmorton. Jim Thogmorton, successively Dean of Men, Dean of Students, and Dean of Alumni Relations, had been called "Dean T" since the 1950s. He and his wife Helen kept in touch with generations of students and are remembered with great love by thousands of alumni.

The new building was completed and completely paid for, and the dedication ceremony was held in 2015.

Other Changes to the Campus

Also in 2014, Linn Memorial Church was updated. The interior was transformed, with more chancel space for musical and theater groups, the pews were removed and replaced with padded chairs, the lighting and sound systems improved. The exterior of the building was tuck-pointed. Most recently, the stained-glass windows have been removed, re-framed and put back in place. The result is a living sanctuary with a long future for both student worship and the worship of the local United Methodist community.

As a result of such gifts as the land for the Besgrove-Hodge Sanctuary and strategic purchases, the Fayette campus has been increased in size by 80%. The master plan developed in the late 90s outlined the areas of the north and east of campus as prime land acquisition areas. Subsequently, the University has purchased 15 properties for a total cost of around $1.5 million that were highlighted in that plan. One key among those was the 2014 purchase of the Rest Home on the corner of Mulberry and Reynolds. This property made possible the development of that site for the Thogmorton Allied Health Building in 2015.

A related change is that, in 2000, alumnus Earl Bates and his wife Sunny bought Coleman Hall, the former home of Central's President, from its then private owners and restored it to its former glory. They make it available to the school for special events.

Another part of the Campaign for the Heart of Central was the renovation of the Stedman Hall of Science. Built in the early 60s, it was a state-of-the-art science classroom building. Today, it is out-dated and badly in need of upgrades. Renovation and remodeling work is to begin in the summer of 2017 and the "new" building will be ready for use in the fall semester of 2018. The Campaign for the Heart of Central is not complete, and funds will still be needed for the completion of the "new" Stedman. Confidence is high that those funds will be available.

The changes to structures on campus ensure that buildings are viable for the present and into the future. The appearance of the campus is also radically changed by the Inman Center, which replaced the old Eyrie, the Thogmorton Center, the renovation of Classic Hall, additions and upgrades to the athletic fields and the proposed "new look" for Stedman Hall. All those are welcome changes. But the character of the campus, with all the shade trees, the trimmed lawns, and the quiet ambiance, has not changed.

6

CELEBRATING A SESQUICENTENNIAL

How often do you get to celebrate a 150th birthday? Every 150 years, right? And how many of us will live that long? In 2004, Central Methodist celebrated 150 years. None of us now living were around in 1854, when the school was started, so we can't remember those early years, but we all have our memories. The Sesquicentennial issue of the *Talon* was full of memories. I could fill pages with the memories of my years at Central – so could you. So, I promise not to do that, just to make the book longer – but I want you to stop reading right now and make a list of some of the great memories you have of your years.

Okay. You've done that. You're now in the mood for remembering how we celebrated the Sesquicentennial. The Alumni Association Board did two things to celebrate.[1]

---

[1] In the interests of full disclosure, the writer was the President of the Alumni Association that year, and most of the material in this chapter is his own memories.

First, they decided to make the Homecoming parade more like "the good old days." Under the leadership of Mike Auchly, the board put together a gorgeous float in the shape of a birthday cake, marking 150 years, crepe paper stuffing and everything. When we drove it in to Fayette for the parade, we discovered that the driver could see only straight ahead, and he would have to make several turns, so two members of the Alumni Board walked backward in front of the float and steered him around the corners. That float was at the head of the parade, just behind the marching band. When the float finished the parade route, the last groups in the parade were just starting out. We had had so much fun, we went around the parade route again. Then we drove the float down to Davis Field and parked it on the grass beyond the track. It was a popular spot for individuals and groups to take pictures in front of all day.

The second thing the Board did was to "sell the Eyrie." No, not the building. But alumnus Bruce Addison had worked with the contractor tearing down the Eyrie and had dozens of small blocks of the Eyrie floor, which he gave the Alumni Board to sell. They sold for $5 each and were sold out long before game-time. An alum said something about dancing on the Eyrie floor and was told that, if she bought 20 of the blocks, they could be inlaid in the rec room floor of her house, and she could dance on the Eyrie floor forever!

There was no student union. The Eyrie was gone, and the new Student and Community Center was not ready for occupancy. Lunch was served under tents down at Davis Field. The Homecoming dance was held on the blocked-off east side of the square. And -- just to make the day perfect – the football team won the game!

Though it was not an official part of the Sesquicentennial Homecoming events, this was a "wow" kind of year. Total gifts to the college in the fiscal year that ended June 30, 2004, exceeded $6.5 million, the greatest total in 150 years. The giving made possible the $750,000 matching grant from the Kresge Foundation and $1.5 million from the Mabee Foundation. In all, from the Campaign for Central, there were 2,500 contributors who made pledges that totaled more than $14,851,750! This meant that the Student and Community Center would be ours – funded entirely with gifts and grants.

For 150 years (longer than that now) Central has been, in President Inman's words, opportunity.[2] Central believes in making education accessible to the maximum number of students. And Central Methodist is people. We are first and foremost a place focused on the strength of relationships. Central Methodist is excellence, values, and achievement. Our graduates have been sought after by employers, and they have lived out the Central Methodist mission of "making a difference in the world" and of demonstrating "ethical leadership and social responsibility." And, finally, Central Methodist *is* success. We are proud of our graduates' high rates in employment and acceptance to post-baccalaureate education. Medical and law schools accept Central graduates at the 95 percent level. Teacher education graduates have, for many years, been employed at nearly the 100 percent level. Athletic training, criminal justice, and nursing graduates claim nearly the same percentage. These results provide evidence of the quality that Central expects and delivers.

---

2 This paragraph is taken nearly verbatim from Marianne Inman, *Talon*, September 2004, p. 2

The Sesquicentennial celebrated all of that, and more.

As we celebrated our sesquicentennial, as we danced and cheered and remembered, as we felt proud of what was happening on the campus, those words reminded us of what Central Methodist means to us and to the broader world in which we live.

7
TRANSFORMING THE CURRICULUM

The Central Methodist University of today is a world apart from the Central Methodist College of 30 years ago. It's like walking into your favorite restaurant that has been closed for renovation. You take in the new paint, new furniture, a more inviting look, and think, "this is really cool." Then you sit down and look at the menu. The offerings are completely changed. Oh, some of the old favorites are still there, but there are many new dishes you never heard of before. That's when you realize that the restaurant world is changing. That's also what happens when you look at the Central Methodist University of today. Things have really changed. Let's begin to examine how much they have changed by a quick look at how they used to be.

The 1998 evaluation report for the North Central Association noted that, for many of the academic areas, there were common concerns. Those were 1) overloading of faculty members, 2) marginal library holdings, computer access, and physical facilities, and 3) a lack of a critical mass of students.[1] The lack of a crucial mass of students has been mostly overcome, thanks to increased enrollment on the Fayette campus. The faculty continues to carry heavy loads, but the overload situation has improved. The computer access issue has also been addressed and improved, and the development of an on-line campus (see below) will move the answer to the concerns for computer access into the 21st century. Physical facilities have been improved (see Chapter 5).

The question about library resources is more in flux. Central Methodist's librarian, Cindy Dudenhoffer, says that they are targeting resources to make dollars stretch as far as possible. Electronic databases make far more resources available at less cost than purchasing books. In a recent year, there were 94,000 usages of the electronic database. That means technical journals available on line, for example, are accessed, and the cost of having print copies of those journals in the library is eliminated. The library, in consultation with the faculty, tries to figure out the wisest use of money. Should they buy expensive books for a program that has six students enrolled, or spend that money for electronic helps? And the curriculum has undergone radical transformation. They try to determine, again with input from faculty, just what is being taught on campus and, therefore, what resources are needed. Then the question becomes what is the most helpful and least expensive way of providing those resources. Many times, the answer is electronic. The circulation of books is down about one-third, but the library is always busy. Students are

---
[1] See the Report of a Visit to Central Methodist College, March 2-4, 1998 for the Commission on Institutions of Higher Education of the North Central Association of Colleges and Schools

clustered around the computer work stations, where in an earlier era, they would have been in the stacks or reading print copies of journals.

Curriculum Revision and Transformation

As of the time of this writing, the curriculum has been revised to better reflect the mission and values of Central Methodist and to clarify what a liberal arts education looks like in today's world. There is a common core curriculum, a 32-hour set of courses required for all students. These courses focus on character development and the formation of the self. There are two freshman courses to orient students to university life and focus on skills for success at the university level. "Foundation" classes are skills-oriented. They include wellness, freshman writing, oral communications, math/algebra/statistics, and advanced writing. "Understanding Human Nature" classes are in the areas of social science, leadership, literature, valuing of social science, and exploring the nature of the universe.

The core curriculum reflects a transformation in the curriculum for at least two reasons. First, it emphasizes the importance of character development. Second, it emphasizes the importance of skills necessary for success at university. Because Central draws so many students who are the first in their family to attend university, because many students do not understand that a university is about more than just gaining information for a degree, and because many students do not have the necessary skills to succeed at university, these foundation courses provide a general introduction to the meaning of life in today's society and how to succeed in this world. This is a radical departure from earlier years at Central where students just started taking classes. Even though some of those classes were pre-requisites, they did not deal with personal growth or exploration of life.

The course listing in the curriculum has also transformed over the past thirty-plus years. Central Methodist, like all other educational institutions, runs on its curriculum offerings. Curriculum is market-driven, so one of the major transformations has been in the curriculum, both to deal with the critical issues of character development and to respond to a changing market. The table below shows how radically the curriculum has changed.

1985 Offerings	2015 Offerings
Art	
Accounting	Accounting
Administration	Athletic Training
Biology	Biology
Marine Biology	Marine Biology
	Molecular Science
	Pre-Health Sciences
	Wildlife Ecology and Conservation
Economics	Business
Chemistry	Chemistry
	Child Development
	Communication
Computer Science	Computer Science
	Criminal Justice
Education	Education

1985 Offerings	2015 Offerings
Early Childhood	Early Childhood
Elementary	Elementary
Junior High	Middle School
High School	Special Education
English	English
Earth Science	Environmental Science
	Exercise Science
Health Sciences	
History	History
	Interdisciplinary Studies
Mathematics	Mathematics
Modern Languages (French, German, Spanish)	
Music	Music
Applied Music	
Music Education	Music Education
	Music Ministry
Nursing	Nursing
Philosophy	Philosophy
	Physics
Political Science	Political Science
Psychology	Psychology
Physical Education	
Religion	Religion
	Religion and Church Leadership
Sociology and Anthropology	Sociology
Speech and the Dramatic Arts	Theatre Arts
	Sports Management
	Applied Behavior Analysis
	RN to BSN (from CGES)

Some courses (or areas) have been dropped, usually because of fewer students. Many others have been added. The additions reflect the changing world in which we live, and the differences in training for careers in that world. Majors with the highest enrollments (as of the Fall of 2015) include teacher education, nursing, biology, business and accounting, athletic training, music, and criminal justice.

In addition, both listings included interdisciplinary or specialty programs. These included (in 1985) Public Service, Science Education, and Social Science Education. For 2015, they included an Accelerated MBA program, Honors Program, Military Science, Pre-Engineering, Pre-Health Professions, Pre-Law, and Pre-Ministry. The 2015 lists also included 12 Associate Degree Programs. Graduate programs are considered in the next chapter.

President Inman, in an interview with the *Talon*,[2] indicated that educational institutions need always to be looking where there is student need. She said we have to offer programs and services that either no one else offers, or that we can offer better than anybody else can. Those programs are what the school markets to let the world know the excellent outcomes our students have always had.

Destination Programs

Among the things we do better are what President Inman called "destination programs." A destination program is one that is basic to campus offerings and that is core to the curriculum. There are three main areas of destination

---

[2] *Talon*, September, 2004, pp. 26-27

programs at CMU – music, education, and health studies.

The first is music. Music, and particularly music education, has always been a strength at Central. A look at the number of high school music teachers and band directors who appear at the annual meetings of the Missouri Music Educators Association displays that strength to the world. Central offers music participation on a level not available at other small colleges. When asked what that last statement meant, Dr. Dori Waggoner, the Dean of the Conservatory, explained that many small colleges don't have marching bands or concert bands (though they may have pep bands or jazz bands) because those larger ensembles are expensive. Central Methodist University has invested in those programs because they add to the culture and identity of the school. One example of that identity is the iconic picture of the marching band at the "Mud Bowl" in St. Louis, and the national coverage that picture received.

At present, the conservatory offers 6 majors: Bachelor of Arts in Music, Bachelor of Music in Vocal Performance, Bachelor of Music in Instrumental Performance, Bachelor of Music Education, Bachelor of Music in Music Ministry (a new degree, which has 3 enrollees at the present) and the Master of Music Education. The latter is a practitioner's degree which meets only in the summer (to fit the schedules of music educators) and has about 25 enrollees.

The recent addition of a major in music ministry is a natural progression for serving a specific need in the church. Music leaders were saying things like "I know how to conduct a choir, or an orchestra, but I don't feel comfortable with praise bands, or planning worship. Help!" This program also strengthens relationships between the university and the church.

In addition, the conservatory has an outreach program with band days and music camps. Band days are both a service and a fund-raiser. They require the services of the entire music faculty and all the music majors for that day. The year 2016 was the 52nd band day. These days draw between 40 and 50 schools, many of them with Central alumni as directors. They serve both large and small schools, so Central intentionally hires judges who understand small schools. Competition is in marching, field, drum line, and color guard categories. Parking is a major problem, because some schools bring not only busses, but also semi-trucks to carry equipment and instruments. However, the return for the university, as well as skill development for the competing schools, is well worth the effort.

Music camps are held in the summer for both band and choral groups. New is a music ministry camp, dealing with contemporary worship music. There is also a color guard camp. These are a source of income, a service to those who attend, and a potential recruiting tool for the University.

In addition, there is the tradition of excellence in music communicated to the world. There are so many names associated with that tradition that to mention any would leave out a dozen others who should have been named. But the tradition continues. Dr. Waggoner said "We accept students from all music backgrounds, figure out where they are, and move them forward."

There is also a continued relationship with alumni. Recently, the Conservatory discovered an alum who was struggling with teaching. They located another alum teaching about 30 minutes away and recruited him as a mentor.

The spirit of helpfulness is a part of the Central tradition, not only for music, as in this case, but in other departments as well. Alums also help Central find students for the future.

Finally, the music tradition at Central found expression when the Chorale sang at the 2016 General Conference of the United Methodist Church in Portland, Oregon. More recently the choir made another national tour in Washington, D.C..

A second destination program is teacher education. Central has a long history of influence in the field of education. In 1909, Central helped establish the Missouri Department of Education and to build criteria for teaching credentials. Taking together the Fayette campus and all the regional locations, 40 percent of enrollment is in teacher education. As of the spring of 2005, Central offered 20 different certifications at the Fayette campus, covering various combinations of early childhood, elementary, middle and high school. It also offers a Bachelor of Science in Child Development, geared to help students build private preschool businesses. The newest certification is in special education.[3] These degrees are also offered at satellite locations, as we will explore in more depth in the following chapter.

The Master of Education is designed primarily for the growth of educational professionals already working in the field. It is available at the Fayette campus, at Mineral Area Community College, CMU in St. Louis, State Fair Community College, North Central Missouri College, and East Central Missouri Community College. It has been approved for online implementation by the Higher Learning Commission.

Students coming to Central to study to become teachers know that they will get excellent preparation and will have

---
3 *Talon*, Spring 2005, p. 12

excellent job opportunities when they graduate. At the time of this writing, Central had virtually a 100 percent placement rate of teachers coming out of our programs. This is, first of all, a vote of confidence by school districts in the quality of their education and preparation, and second, a great marketing tool for recruiting more excellent students.

Both those programs, music and teacher education, have been long-standing components in Central's success and influence across the state of Missouri and beyond. The third destination, health professions, is relatively new in the curriculum.

There are three components to this destination. Central has had a long tradition of excellence in the pre-medical area. We continue to have about a 95 percent acceptance rate at medical schools, a vote of confidence in the academic preparation of young men and women.

The second component of the health professions is the nursing program. This actually began in 1974, under the leadership of Dr. John Smart. In the beginning, it was an associate degree, approved by the Missouri State Board. It was fully in place in 1974. The degree program began in the 1980s, and the associates program was phased out effective in 1995. The two year RN-BSN degree completion program moved to the College of Graduate and Extended Studies (see chapter 8). The degree program is now online, and there are several hundred in the program each year. That program was accredited in the spring of 2006 by CCNE.

The Masters program in nursing began in 2006-2007. It is a clinical nurse leader program, one which is newly developed. The program is designed to develop leadership in the profession for people still working "at the bedside."

In 2011-2012, the Masters program in Nursing Education was started. The emphasis here is on nurses moving to a higher level of teaching, where they would need a degree at least one level above the students. In the near future, Central will probably be offering a Ph.D. in nursing education.

Other New Programs

Two new programs which recently received candidacy status are occupational therapy assistants and physical therapy assistants. In order to gain certification status for these programs, the complete preparation needs to be on paper – all the lesson plans, all the tests, everything – before the program is even evaluated. Teaching occupational therapy requires a master's degree. Therapy assistants, who have completed the program and are working in the field, carry out a plan of care developed by a registered therapist.

The opening of the Thogmorton Center for Allied Health has been a major boost to the health programs. Finally, there is room to expand the programs. Students will be able to do part, at least, of their simulation on campus and not have to go to Columbia or Marshall for that.

Another relatively new addition to the curriculum is Criminal Justice, which started in 1994. The addition of Terri Haack to the faculty in 2003 allowed for an expansion of the program from basic classes, to include crime scene investigation, juvenile justice, serial crime, and (just recently) cybercrime. Courses are taught hands-on to Missouri State Highway Patrol standards. Currently there are 64 students in the program. Ninety-eight percent of the graduates get jobs. That's the broad picture. Beyond course names, there is the reality that criminal justice is a lot about helping people. Students almost 100% are motivated by the need to help people. As one student said, "I want to make a difference by working in the correctional system."4 It is a reality in today's world that one bad decision can put you in prison for life. Criminal justice students at Central Methodist can see beyond punishment to helping people change their lives. At the same time, it takes courage and personal commitment to do justice in a day when the justice system is under such intense scrutiny. Students learn both critical thinking skills and the practical application of the classroom to the real world.

The Spring 2015 *Talon* reported on the attendance of Central students at the National Conference of the American Criminal Justice Association. The *Talon* said, "as has become an expectation, they took first or second in every event they entered."5 They brought home four trophies, the only school to take home more trophies than the number of students who attended! A look at the full trophy case outside the department offices in T Berry Smith shows how much Central Methodist students have contributed to the image of the university in the criminal justice field.

When asked if there were really a lot of jobs in the field, Professor Haack shared a document titled "What Can I Do with a Criminal Justice Degree?" The document contained 2¼ pages, double columns, single-spaced, with job opportunities in almost every department of government, as well as business and education.

Athletic Training is another relatively new program. This is a specialization of sports medicine that, in collaboration

---

4 Interview with Terri Hauck, June 27, 2017

5 *Talon*, Spring 2015, p. 43

with physicians, works at prevention (wellness, etc.), emergency care, rehab (orthopedic) and clinical diagnosis. In 1992, this was a minor. In 1996, it became a major. In 2000, it was nationally accredited and became a degree program.

Athletic Training has a pre-professional program which prepares a student to enter the professional program. Currently, there are 30-40 students in pre-professional. Meeting the pre-professional requirements does not automatically guarantee admission into the professional degree program. There are 40 students currently in the professional program. Because of accreditation requirements, this program is now transitioning to a graduate program.

Career opportunities include athletic training, schools, clinics, hospitals, commercial and governmental work places. For example, Boeing hires 90+ athletic trainers. The military, Amazon, sports medicine, all hire many trainers. At one point, the St. Louis Rams had a graduate of the Central athletic training program, which enabled the school to have interns on their staff. The Rams move to Los Angeles hurt that internship program. Some eighty percent of CMU's graduates go on to get a Masters. That is because many of them want to teach, which today requires at least a Masters.

Two other graduate programs which do not fit easily into the categories mentioned above are the Master of Science in Mathematics which requires thirty-one hours of coursework in theoretical and computational mathematics.

The second is the Master of Science in Clinical Counseling. It prepares practitioners to function as professional counselors who meet the State of Missouri's requirements as a Licensed Professional Counselor. This program is available in Park Hills, Sedalia, Columbia, and Maryland Heights.

And now, in what may be the biggest transformation of all, Central Methodist University is going digital. The Board recently committed $1,000,000 to make Central the third college or university in the state to do so. The basic infrastructure has been established, faculty have begun receiving training, and every student will have an i-Pad given to them when they register. Board members report that the faculty who have been trained gave an enthusiastic demonstration of how the i-pads can be used in their classes to facilitate learning. As one person said, "we're going to be teaching them the way they learn." The transformation won't happen overnight, of course, but it is well on the way.

Curriculum offerings have changed so much to keep in step with the needs of students that their listings can truly be called a transformation. The structure of the curriculum has changed, the appearance of listings has changed, and the character has been lifted. Not only does the curriculum reflect more carefully the needs of the market in today's economy, but also it aims toward building thoughtful character into the practitioners.

8

THE COLLEGE OF GRADUATE AND EXTENDED STUDIES

As is the case with many of the best ideas for goods and services, the College for Graduate and Extended Studies began with a complaint. In a conversation with President Joe Howell, the President of the Mineral Area Community College complained that Southeast Missouri State would not give them attention for the needs of their students, specifically for helping build on their Associate degrees to move to the baccalaureate level. President Howell said "we'll help," without knowing everything that promise would mean. That conversation was in the fall of 1989 and proved to be the beginning of the first public-private partnership and the first 2 + 2 program in the state of Missouri. Actually, there are two different stories circulating about the beginning of these partnerships. The other is that President Howell asked Braxton Rethwisch how Central could make an extra million dollars a year. Braxton replied, "well, there is this paper

I'm working on." There is probably some truth in both stories. In any event, the door was opened for the 2 + 2 program, which evolved into the College for Graduate and Extended Studies.[1]

With the commitment made, the next question was, how do we carry it out? President Howell called on Braxton Rethwisch to help work out the details and support for the program. Not only had Braxton been working on a paper about such a program, but he had worked in the eastern part of Missouri for years, recruiting students, building relationships. With years of experience in the area, he knew many of the people who would need to be involved, and the needs of the communities they served. Because of the financial situation Central faced, Dr. Howell wanted to house the program in a church basement or basements. Braxton argued that the program would appear more professional and attractive if it were in an academic setting. So that decision was made.

There was clearly a need. Students who were already holding an Associate degree would love to carry their studies through to the logical conclusion of a four year degree, namely, a Bachelor's. A program such as a 2 + 2 would mean they would not have to leave home and/or job in order to pursue their education. They could work on a degree at less cost and disruption of family and/or work life. It was a win-win situation. Mineral Area College was asked to provide one furnished office, up to five furnished general purpose classrooms, and one computer lab. Central Methodist took

---
1 2+2 refers to a program where a student attends a community college for two years and then takes courses at a four-year college for another two years (or more) to complete the work for a bachelor's degree.

on the rest. The program offered up to five separate courses each eight-week term, with five terms offered each year. The classes met in three-hour sessions for two nights a week.

The Mineral Area site opened in August of 1989 with 50 students. Those students graduated in 1991. This was the beginning of a public-private venture which has met the needs of hundreds of students and proved to be a financial dividend for Central Methodist. We will explore the details of several ways in which that happened in the following pages.

In order for the program to work in an area, there must be qualified faculty. Sometimes that means the use of a full-time faculty person from the Fayette campus teaching a particular course (either in person or online). For the most part, it means adjunct faculty, using persons with the necessary knowledge and skills who live in the area, know the community, and may know the students as well. There is also the need for an appropriate balance of the assessment of needs, the availability of resources to meet the needs, marketing the program, and customer satisfaction. Finally, there is the issue of compliance with government regulations. Dr. Rita Gulstad, CMU Provost who has leadership responsibilities for CGES, says that 80% of her time is taken up with compliance (The other 50% of her time is spent on more interesting things!!).

The Growth of Extended Studies

Extended studies refers to a grouping of programs, including 2+2, online classes, dual credit courses in high schools, and graduate programs. With some exceptions, these may be held on or off the Fayette campus.

Today, some 27 years after the program opened at Mineral

Area College, it has expanded to 16 sites in Missouri (counting all the St. Louis sites as one, and the same with the Kansas City Metropolitan Community Colleges). In addition, there are programs offered at Southeastern Illinois College in Harrisburg, Illinois; Southeastern Community College in Burlington, Iowa; Northeast Iowa Community College in Dubuque, Iowa; Iowa Western Community College in Council Bluffs, Iowa; Indian Hills Community College in Ottumwa, Iowa; Kaskaskia College in Centralia, Illinois; and Rend Lake College in Ina, Illinois. (Note that in the partnerships outside of Missouri, Central Methodist does not offer traditional classroom courses, but provides on-line courses leading to a Bachelor's degree.) Most of these sites offer around a dozen programs in undergraduate studies. Master's programs in Education, Clinical Counseling, Music Education, Nursing (Clinical Leader) or Nursing (Nurse Educator) are offered, depending on location.[2] As of the 25th anniversary of CGES, those programs were:[3]

Graduate Programs

Location	Spring Enrollment	Programs
Fayette	48	Master of Education, Master of Music Ed.
St. Louis (Dorsett)	28	Master of Education
Park Hills	50	Master of Science in Clinical Counseling, Master of Education
Poplar Bluff	6	Master of Education

[2] "CGES at 25, all grown up and going strong," *Talon*, Fall 2014, p. 35.

[3] As of Spring 2014. Source: Minutes of the Board of Trustees meeting, February 14 and 15.

Location	Spring Enrollment	Programs
Online	48	Master of Science in Nursing
Union	2	Master of Education

Undergraduate Programs

Location	Spring Enrollment	Programs
Neosho	5	2 courses
Clinton	35	12 areas
Waynesville	25	11 areas
Sedalia	119	12 areas
Lake of the Ozarks	61	12 areas
Linn	9	2 areas
Trenton	4	2 areas
Macon	1	4 areas
Rolla	2	RN to BSN
Columbia	776	4 areas
Fayette	139	
Union	160	12 areas
Poplar Bluff	134	10 areas
Park Hills	316	18 areas
St. Louis	61	Child Development
St. Louis (Dorsett)	150	RN to BSN, Business, Psychology
St. Peters	33	RN to BSN
St. Louis, St. Anthony's	89	RN to BSN
Hillsboro	11	RN to BSN
St. Louis (Mercy)	28	RN to BSN
Online	361	10 areas

The *Talon* reported that, in the fall of 2014, more than 4,600 students were taking coursework through the College of Graduate and Extended Studies[4] (CGES).

In nearly every case, relationships with these partner institutions were the result of on-site visits by President Inman and Dr. Gulstad (now the Provost of the University).

Unique Locations

Not all of the CGES locations and extended sites operate the same way. Some have actual physical presence, others operate online, still others have unique relationships. The Columbia location, for example, has an office and classrooms. The University of Missouri is a big supporter and sends many students to the Central location in Columbia. The majority of the students here are non-degree seeking. Originally, most of the students were in math courses. They were having trouble dealing with math concepts in large classes at Mizzou and needed more individual instruction to master those concepts. In a setting with smaller classes and some special attention, they flourished, and went back to the University for their degree. Now the Columbia location also includes child development and business courses at the location in the Forum Shopping Center. In 2013, CMU added one large classroom room to provide space for the new Accelerated Bachelor of Science in Nursing program. As of Fall, 2015, 48 classes were being taught at the Columbia location and there were 592 students enrolled. Most of them (77%) were classroom only students.

State Fair Community College in Sedalia is another physical location which offers a unique service to the State

---
4 Fall, 2014, p. 32

Fair campus. Because of the partnership with Central Methodist, State Fair Community College now is able to provide free personal counseling for their students. The Clinical Counseling Center is staffed with graduate students who are in their final year of CMU's counseling program. In this win-win situation, State Fair Community College met a perceived need among their students for personal counseling. CMU graduate students found a place to do clinical work under the supervision of their instructor and clinical director. Through the relationship with State Fair, CMU also works with the Lake of the Ozarks and Clinton sites.

Central Methodist University in Saint Louis began in Spring 2010 in partnership with the Institute for Professional Development. It became a stand alone CMU program in June 2013. The headquarters is a group of offices and classrooms in Maryland Heights. Several two year public colleges and medical centers are affiliated with CMU in St. Louis: St. Charles Community College; Jefferson College (Arnold); Barnes-Jewish-Christian Learning Institute (St. Louis); Mercy St. Louis Hospital; Mercy Jefferson Hospital (Festus); this became Jefferson Regional Medical Center (Festus); St.Anthony's Medical Center (St. Louis); SSM Health Care (St. Louis). There are programs in several hospital settings, allowing RNs to earn their Bachelor of Science in Nursing in their professional setting. In addition, the St. Louis center offers bachelor's degree programs in Business, Child Development, Health Sciences, Psychology, Nursing (above), and the Master of Education. Some 450 students were enrolled at the St. Louis sites at the time of this reporting.

There are so-called "overlay" programs for students in the 2+2 programs at CMU in St. Louis and CMU in Columbia. One such program is online courses used to fulfill degree requirements. Some students are not affiliated with a location (e.g., St. Louis or Columbia) and are designated as independent or online only students. In some cases, degrees can be achieved with totally online courses.

Graduate Studies

CGES offers six master's degrees in Education, Music Education, Clinical Counseling, Nursing-Nurse Educator, Nursing-Clinical Nurse Leader, and Mathematics.

CGES has approximately 300 adjunct faculty members who are often employees of our partner institutions and professionals in their fields. There are also 10 full-time faculty members in the graduate and extended programs.

In the fall of 2015, there were 2468 students enrolled in CGES programs. Of these, 1027 were in 2+2 programs, 485 in CMU St. Louis, 592 in CMU Columbia, and 364 independents.

At its beginning in 1989, CGES enrolled 28 undergraduate students. In 2015, that number had grown to 2457 undergraduates and 261 graduate students.[5]

The graduate program also comes under the CGES umbrella. This began in 1996 with the Master of Education degree. Graduate courses were developed and added to the curriculum in response to perceived needs. The Master of Science in Critical Counseling degree was first offered in 2004, the Master of Science in Nursing – Clinical Nurse

---
5 These figures are taken from Central Methodist University Overview, Fall 2015, p. 9

Leader in 2008, the Master of Music Education in 2013, the Master of Science in Nursing – Nurse Educator in 2014, and the Master of Science in Mathematics in 2015. Dr. John J. Carter is the Director of Graduate Studies and reports to Dr. Gulstad. Within the CGES faculty, there are approximately 40 adjunct faculty devoted to the graduate program.

Online Teaching

One of the keys to the success of CGES is the use of technology. In the mid-1990s, CMU had some faculty (in particular Prof. John Flanders) teaching online. In 2015, Central Methodist now offers over 600 classes on line, with 13 degree programs, two of which are graduate. Some 80% of CMU students take a class (or classes) on line. This figure includes both the Fayette campus and partner institutions.

The desirable features of online teaching are obvious. The first is that you don't need to meet a class in a particular place at a particular time. For students who are working full-time, raising a family, and/or caring for older family members, to be able to take a course when they have time and energy is a blessing. The downside of that is that all those other demands on their time and energy mean that they are not always as alert when they work online as one would hope. The second desirable feature is cost. It is much cheaper to take a course online from the comfort of your home than to drive to another location (and pay higher tuition costs). The two C's, cost and convenience, help explain the popularity of online teaching/learning and Central's success in reaching this market.

Sixteen weeks of class hours are covered in eight weeks, which also helps explain the popularity of this option. Lectures can be videoed and posted on the website. Prof. Flanders' courses, for example, are based on a textbook, usually an e-textbook, that has assignments and quizzes for each chapter. In addition, CMU requires discussion forums for each class.

The downside of online courses is also obvious – it is the lack of interaction, both between students and faculty and between students in the course. Being in the same room with the faculty person and other students sparks learning in a different way from that in which one engages primarily with a computer. But Dr. Gulstad also affirms the belief that there is more interaction with students in online programs. She also says that studies show online students tend to be better students than those in similar "seated" programs. It is also true that the faculty person never really knows if the student has read the textbook. Again, Dr. Gulstad says that assessments "make it pretty apparent if a student is engaging with the course material...which may not be a textbook anymore." Most conscientious students will, one hopes, make every effort to do so. But time and energy factors enter into this, as well.

Clearly, technology – and online courses – is here to stay. Once you let that particular genie out of the bottle, you can never stuff it back in again. A comment from one of the Trustees shows that 80% of the income for CGES comes from online courses. That is a not insignificant contribution to the financial health of the institution!

How Did CGES Become So Successful?

The key to the success of CGES is innovation. Dr. Gulstad and her staff listen to what people tell them. What are the needs in an area served by a community college? As that area develops economically, what are the needs for training? Are trained nurses the pressing need? Or, as in the case with State Fair Community College, is it clinical counseling? Once the needs are identified, the question becomes, "will the students come?" CMU is recognized as being the most flexible university working with community colleges. The school is also recognized for being honest about what it can and can't do, keeping its word, the quality of the education it offers, and being economically effective. That's a pretty good reputation to have. Central can also change programs around, depending on the community need. As community needs change, so can the kinds of programs that Central offers. One interesting item – CMU is the only nationally accredited +2 program in music education!

Central's online studies are getting closer to being available nationwide. That's because, in the spring of 2015, Central was granted institutional participant status by the National Council for State Authorization Reciprocity Agreements, or SARA. This allows Central to offer online degrees to residents of SARA affiliated states. With the addition of SARA member states, CMU can now offer online degrees in 42 states.[6] As of this writing, CMU offers 14 Bachelor's degree programs online, along with two options of its Master of Science in Nursing degree, and the Master of Science in Mathematics.

---

6 *Talon*, Spring 2015, p. 34

Issues still to be resolved include the question of branding. Who is Central Methodist? How do prospective students recognize us and want to participate? Another is the question of how to relate to alumni from this program. The extension centers are now recognized as part of the university, but that does not mean that students in those centers identify with Central Methodist University in the same way that students on the Fayette campus do. The Alumni Association has struggled with this question for over a decade (at the time of this writing) and has not yet been able to find a clear answer.

High School Dual Credit

In 1995, the Missouri Interactive Telecommunications Education Network (MIT-E)[7] came together. This was a consortium of five school districts (Slater, Glasgow, New Franklin, Pilot Grove, and Bunceton) and Central Methodist University, plus Southwestern Bell Telephone, and Mid-Missouri Telephone, to provide dual credit through interactive television. Central can teach ITV (Interactive Television) high school courses, dual-credit courses and courses on the East Central Missouri Community College campus.

The program has expanded to now serve 100 or more schools. Dr. Rita Gulstad, CMU Provost, announced that Central is one of six colleges and universities to gain first-time accreditation from the National Alliance of Concurrent Enrollment Partnerships (NACEP). "Dual Credit Program Gains National Accreditation" News Release, Central

---

[7] The material on dual credit programs and technology is taken from the 1998-99 Self Study, p. 79

Methodist University, May 4, 2015. The material about accreditation and what it means comes from the news release. Central Methodist also becomes one of only seven four-year private colleges in Missouri with NACEP accreditation.

The Dual Credit program allows qualified high school students to enroll in approved classes and receive both high school and college credit. This gives them an early start in fulfilling college requirements at many colleges and universities, including CMU. In the spring of 2015, there were approximately 1500 students enrolled in dual credit courses, representing some 90 school districts, according to the program's coordinator, Peggy O'Connell. The variety of courses offered includes Principles of Accounting, General Biology, Human Anatomy, Chemistry, Criminal Justice, Structured Programming, Communication Skills, Child Development, Intro to World Literature, World Geography, College Algebra, Calculus and Analytical Geometry, Physics, Sociology, and others.

Typically, CMU courses are taught by college-approved high school teachers who meet CMU qualifications. NACEP has developed the only national set of quality standards for dual credit partnerships. Those standards assure that the course content and expectations for student work in high schools match the standards of the sponsoring university, according to Dr. Gulstad. NACEP accreditation also validates the quality of CMU's program to the participating high schools.

Challenges

"Bricks and clicks" is a key phrase for summarizing CGES. Dr. Gulstad says that institutions offering online programs are most often considered to have quality when they have an actual campus. The actual campus (Fayette, in this case) creates a brand of quality. That is an intangible which almost has to exist, even though it is sometimes difficult to quantify.

An external force is cost – and keeping the cost down. As in any other market-driven enterprise, customers are looking for the best possible product at the lowest possible cost. At the same time, the institution has to make a profit in order to stay in existence and offer the services that the customers want. This will always be a delicate balancing act.

The role of faculty has changed dramatically because of online teaching and other tasks that were outlined above. The emphasis is more and more on the needs of the student, and meeting those needs in creative and meaningful ways. Faculty don't have time to do everything that needs to be done. "Publish or perish" is gone for schools like CMU. There is little or no time for research and publishing. The demand on the faculty time for interaction with students, on the one hand, and more administrative work on the other, makes the traditional faculty role obsolete.

A challenge that continues to elude efforts to deal with it is the continued relationship with the alumni of extended programs. A student from a location miles away from Fayette, or even in another state, does not have the same feelings about Central Methodist University as an alumnus from the Fayette campus. They may hold a degree from Central Methodist, but they don't have the same "family" feeling, or loyalty of a student who lived on the Fayette campus. That's natural. The question is, how does the University relate to those students as "alumni" to whatever degree?

Finally, it will always be important to meet professional requirements. Courses of study have to meet the requirements of accrediting agencies if the university wants to stay in business. That explains the 80% of Dr. Gulstad's time that is spent on compliance with regulations.

A new challenge that is beginning to keep the administration awake at night is the fact that Central has been so successful that public universities are wanting to start extension programs of their own and grab a share of the market. We will need to continue to run hard, just to stay in place.

Another challenge is assessment of student learning, an issue raised by the evaluation team in 1998. The degree-completion programs serve a student population with different backgrounds and experiences in a non-residential setting. Since 2008, Central Methodist has had in place a strong assessment program that does not need to take into consideration differences by location/program/demographic. Students are prepared for programs of study with the same learning outcomes and assessment measures.

Photographs

Marianne Inman, Ph.D. President, 1995-2013

Photographs

Dr. Joseph Geist and Denise Haskamp,
Curators of the Ashby-Hodge Gallery of Art

Criminal Justice students working at the
Besgrove-Hodge Sanctuary

Photographs

President Inman strikes the first blow in the demolition of the Eyrie

The completed Inman Student and Community Center

Photographs

Classic Hall

Thogmorton Center for Allied Health

Photographs

Conference on the Lawn

Working out the Challenges for Tomorrow

Photographs

President and Mrs. Drake having fun at Homecoming

CGES – Columbia, Mo location

Photographs

Roger Drake, Ed.D., President, 2013 -----

9
WE BECOME A UNIVERSITY

So far in this book, we've talked about changes. In coming chapters, we'll be talking about more changes. Most of those changes were – and are – transformational. The change that expresses all that transformation is the change of name for the institution – from college to university. Wait. A University? Central? In Fayette? How can that be?

For over a century, Central was simply known as Central College. In the early 1960s, it was discovered that the name had never been registered with the State of Missouri, and so the school technically did not have a legal name. In the process of obtaining that State recognition, the word "Methodist was added to the name" and we became Central Methodist College.

In the 1990s, President Inman asked Trustee Tad Perry to form a committee to look at the question of changing our name (and status) to a university. The committee struggled with two key questions. First, is the structure of the campus different enough to justify the name change? If so, does the title reflect the difference? Does "university" reflect a different structure? And, second, is there any public relations value in a name change?

With regard to the first question, it was clear that the campus had changed. By "campus" here is meant the structure under which the school operates, not just the look of the Fayette campus (though it had changed as well). The table of organization showed a College of Liberal Arts and Sciences (CLAS), primarily the Fayette location, and a College of Graduate and Extended Studies (CGES), primarily the other locations where Central offered academic courses, plus the graduate program. And, the school was offering graduate degrees in several areas, which is another criterion for being called a university. Did the title reflect the changes in structure? The answer to that question seemed clear – it did not.

What about the public relations value of a name change? "University" connotes something more than "college" does in today's climate of community colleges. While Central is proud of its working relationships with so many community colleges, there was a desire to distinguish ourselves as different from a community college. Why? There was some feeling that a name change would benefit student recruitment. And it is true that, since the name change, enrollment on the Fayette campus has increased. That, of course, leads to a further question: post hoc, ergo propter hoc? That is, did the enrollment increase because of the name change, or is the name change simply one of many factors? The name change almost certainly helps in faculty recruitment. Newly graduated persons seeking a teaching position will tend to gravitate toward a university, rather than toward a college.

So, the committee was ready to report that the key questions about changing the name to Central Methodist University were answered in the affirmative. Then came discussion about what the new name should be. That discussion centered around the term "Methodist." After much discussion, the decision was made that we should keep the name "Methodist" for several reasons. First, the name is an honest reflection of our heritage. Our founders were Methodist ministers, and the aim of the college was to be the only Methodist school in the state. When, in the early 1960s, it was discovered that the name Central College had never been registered with the state, the curators chose to submit the name Central Methodist College for registration. So keeping the word "Methodist" in the title would reflect a tradition and a heritage. Second, the institution has a relationship with the Missouri Conference of the United Methodist Church, and receives financial support from the conference, and from individual churches. "Methodist" is in the Central DNA, and needed to be reflected in the school's name.

The Board of Curators (as they were then known) received the committee's report and voted to proceed. The first step was to clear the use of the new name with the state. This was done for legal reasons. The state agreed that the name "Central Methodist University" was not in use, and the administration registered it with the state. The same was true for social media – the name did not have proprietary status on social media, and it was immediately bought for the website, etc. Faculty were polled about the use of the name, as were alumni. Both groups approved, though there was minority dissent. One alumna said to my wife and myself that she did not like the change. She wanted to keep "Central

Methodist College," because that was the school from which she graduated. My wife's response was that, for us, the name had already changed once (when it became Central Methodist College) and one more wasn't going to bother us!

So we became Central Methodist University. One more step in the excitement around the transformation of Central. As one alum said, "we're playing with the big kids now." And so we move into the future, not only "playing with the big kids," but more than holding our own with them.

10

Transforming Student Success

What does it mean for a student to succeed? As Joy Flanders said, half serious and half joking, "they graduate." That's an important indicator, to be sure. One recent report reminds us that an important measurement of success is a "6-year graduation rate." That is, what is the percentage of entering students who graduate in 6 years or less? That report listed the percentage of students graduating in 6 years or less, by the entering freshmen years. The numbers for Central Methodist are instructive.

    2004 -- 45.1%

    2005 -- 42.6%

    2006 -- 49.8%

    2007 -- 40.0%

    2008 -- 51.7%[1]

---

[1] Central Methodist University Overview, Fall 2015, p. 6

The percentages seem discouragingly low. However, it is important to remember that students may attend more than one college or university before they graduate. They may change majors, drop out for a year or two for financial reasons, and other factors. So, while the statistics may be discouraging, they are also somewhat confusing.

Success could also mean making B grades instead of C grades. Other indicators might include such things as "they feel good about themselves," "they've learned to think critically," "they have a sense of belonging to something bigger than themselves," or "they got a job." Any or all of them would be important to a particular student. How does Central Methodist stand out in terms of facilitating student success? Particular attention is given to this from matriculation to graduation, and on to employment.

Center for Teaching and Learning

On the Fayette campus, the Center for Teaching and Learning is a key factor in student success. The program began with Title III – first generation students. In 1990, Maryann Rustmeyer came on board with a study skills component and developmental education background. The aim of the program, which developed slowly as student needs became clearer, was to do whatever was necessary to help students succeed. In the early years of the program, it was diffused throughout the campus. Tutors were hired by the academic divisions, and they met everywhere (or anywhere) on campus. This caused a lot of confusion for students. Where are we supposed to meet? With whom do we meet? The result was less than satisfactory in terms of student success. The best part of the program in those early days was study halls for the football players in Stedman Hall. It was suggested that this portion succeeded because the coaches were promoting it and, at least to some degree, monitoring the progress of the students.

In 2000, the Center began to hire the tutors. This allowed for more consistency in the program and clarity about where they were meeting. Then, in 2003, Dr. Rustmeyer was involved in an accident in which her car was hit by a truck, and she was sidelined for a considerable period of time. Her absence convinced administrators that the Center was a program which was needed for student success. When the Ashby-Hodge Gallery moved from the first floor of the Library, the Center took over a large part of that floor.

The question, "how do you deal with learning disabilities in the classroom?" led to an emphasis on student success. Joy Flanders joined the program with a portfolio on intentional support. One new emphasis was on testing. Students with learning disabilities often struggle with the pressure of test-taking because they are not "programmed" to operate in that pressure setting. So they come to the Center to take tests in a calmer setting. The Center also supervises makeup tests for students who had to be absent when a test was given. This frees up faculty time for working with students on a one-to-one basis. One wonders, in terms of success for these special needs students, how their peers respond to them taking tests in a separate setting. What are the factors complicating community among students? Or do all students "cheer" when there is success for another?

Study halls for athletes also come under the Center's responsibilities. The coaches decide how many hours each athlete needs. This is important for both the coaches and the Center. The coach wants his or her athletes academically eligible to play, obviously. The fact that the coach decides how much time the student-athlete needs puts some teeth in the program so that the Center can demand the required participation.

This chapter began with a comment from Joy Flanders on what success means. We continue with another comment on helping students achieve that success. When asked what she did as a part of the program, Ms. Flanders' response was "whatever it takes." This could mean academic advising – "are you really in the program you need to be?" It could include helping faculty develop strategies for student success in their classrooms. It involves getting students who are struggling, or who are goofing off, back on track. It does involve (I witnessed it happening while we were talking) calling students and reminding them to get up and get to class. It is, as Ms. Flanders said, a last-ditch effort for student success.

One marker for student success is the retention rate, particularly for freshmen. What is the retention from fall to fall? At Central in 2014, that retention rate was 63.9%, according to government regulations. That's not a retention rate that has administration shouting for joy, though it is a rate that is improving slowly. Interestingly, Ms. Flanders said that the student loss is not so much because of grades or social problems, but because of family finances. Some of those students who don't come back the second year drop out to work and save money to re-enroll another year. This statement also helps us understand better the significance of the six-year graduation rate.

Finally, the services for success are now provided for all the Central locations. They serve provisional students,

students on academic probation, re-admits, and references from coaches and other faculty. It's obvious that student success is measured in far different ways than it may have been in earlier decades. The key, reflected in the mission statement, is that Central Methodist University is striving to produce students who believe in themselves, who have a sense of pride in what they do, and who are ready to make a difference in their communities. That goes beyond "making the dean's list," or graduating at any cost.

The James C. Denneny Career Development Center

Last but not least, we come to the Denneny Career Development Center. It was founded by James C. Denneny, Jr., with a mission "to empower students to develop the tools they need to successfully transition from campus life to a professional career path."[2] Simply choosing a major doesn't solidify choices about a career. For example, one pastor said recently in a sermon that he had had nine majors in college! Then he wound up going to seminary. The Career Development Center helps students think carefully about career choices as a part of their education. How does it do this?

First of all, with assessments. The goal here is to help the students discover what they want that they haven't even thought about openly, perhaps, then to help them see the possibilities to which their passion might lead them. What would they like to do?

Second, the Center helps a student to create a resume. This is a part of the learning process in two regards. It helps them develop skills in writing a resume that will attract attention.

---
2 CMU website, "The James C. Denneny, Jr., Career Development Center."

AND, it helps them discover their skills and interests.

These days, many employers want applicants who leave college with at least two internships. The old practice of a "summer job" that might have no relationship to career goals is a thing of the past. For example, my goal was ministry, but I spent my summers working in a filling station and putting up hay after work. No more. Today, the process is internships, which are also academic. An internship is not just a job in a particular field, but also it is learning something for academic credit. Internships help students learn about the field, and if it is really what they want to do. Since many internships are not paid, the Center also works with parents to help them see the importance of the internship for reaching long-term employment goals, as opposed to the short-term satisfaction of some income over the summer. Many companies are looking for graduates who have had at least one, but preferably two, internships in the field where they are looking for a job. So a big part of the Center's work is networking with companies to discover internships for students, and with students, steering them toward internships.

The Center teaches and practices interview skills. As a result, there are a lot of mock interviews, many of them conducted by alumni working in the field in which the student is applying for a position. Sometimes there are direct hires as a result of the mock interview. Nicolette Yevich, the Director of Career Development, shared a story about a student whose mock interviews totally transformed her situation. This young lady was an excellent student with a 4.0 grade average. She was not the leader type, but a good team player. Her career goal was to become a counselor. Ms. Yevich encouraged her to do a mock interview.

The student did poorly on the interview and was devastated. This was the point at which some students give up because they don't have the help and encouragement such as that provided by the Career Development Center.

Ms. Yevich convinced the student to meet with her once a month to deal with issues of resume development and interviewing skills. A year later she had a second mock interview with the same person from the same company – and aced it. The student was a success because the staff at the Center worked with her and transformed her life.

Note that this student gained transferable skills from the process, skills that would make a difference not only in getting started in a career, but all through her life. That is true success.

Practical matters are also important. The Center sponsors etiquette dinners, where students learn professional table manners and how to carry on a conversation, or an interview, while eating lunch or dinner. Professional dress is also stressed. What does one wear for a serious interview? Because some students don't even have the proper kind of dress, the Center keeps a selection of clothing students can wear for mock interviews and/or the real thing.

The activity in a recent semester illustrates all the points mentioned above. In the Fall of 2014, there was a workshop with voice faculty and the Student National Association of Teachers of Singing on "Music Entrepreneurship – Visioning for a Portfolio Career." Then came two informational workshops. The first was an Internship Panel where CMU students spoke about their summer internships. They talked about career benefits, networking, and being more confident in their career path. The second session was with the United

States Marine Corps where students learned about the opportunities in becoming a commissioned officer.

There was a Mock Interview Series, designed to help students be more prepared for the styles and techniques of interviewers. Students were asked the kinds of questions that are a typical part of a job interview. This included a resume critique component. The Etiquette Dinner helped students be aware of the importance of being professional while eating and carrying on a conversation with a prospective employer.

Other workshops included job opportunities led by a special agent from the Drug Enforcement Administration. Dress to Impress workshops looked at style considerations for both men and women. Then in February 2015, the Center hosted its annual Career EXPO where companies came and reserved tables to promote themselves and look for possible hires. All in all, it was a busy semester for Director Nicolette Yevich and her staff.

What does all this add up to? Director Yevich says it is "dreaming a little better for people." Helping people dream for themselves and discover the skills to make that dream come true.

What's the Payoff?

Where does all this support and attention lead? How do we know that students succeed? When you have an entering student with an ACT of 21 and, with guidance and support from faculty, that student is now in law school, you have success. When you have an entering student with an ACT of 21 and that student is now engaged in a career, you have success. Central Methodist can point with pride to those students and many others like them, who have been transformed by their university experience. Of course, it would be wonderful if all entering students had ACT scores in the 30s, but this is the real world. Brilliant students will succeed, for the most part. But real student success, and real satisfaction for faculty and administration, comes from the stories of students like the ones with whom we began this paragraph. Not many schools have that record of success.

11
Transforming Student Life

Resident life is always an adjustment. Freshmen students, particularly those who are first generation and/or come from high schools where they were able to excel without having to work hard, have to learn how to handle their time, how to plan their study schedule so they do not have to "cram" at the last minute. If they also have to juggle work-study or a part-time job, this adds stress to their lives. That has always been true for new students, some of whom have to learn how to study for the first time. Many discover that all the "free" time they seem to have requires some serious decisions about how to use that time to do their studies and still have time for a social life, service activity, and so on.

In addition, Fayette is a small town without the amenities some, if not many students are used to. There is no movie theater, no bowling alley, even the McDonald's has closed (though the Dairy Queen continues to appear to thrive). One has to go to Boonville or Columbia to find a Wal-Mart or a movie.

So what do students do when they have their studies for the day complete? What do they find for a social life?

Student Government Association

Martha (Mattie) Bradley, the current President of the Student Government Association, agreed completely with the material in the introduction to this chapter (above). Her comment was, "we are forced to do things together."[1] Social life depends on students working together to create an environment that enriches their life and university experience.

So student government is the source of a great deal of the life on campus. Their big event is always Homecoming, which they help sponsor and help organize. In recent years, Homecoming has become a much more significant experience for both students and alumni, which says that student government is making a difference.

Other activities include social events. One example is "Wings Night" where chicken wings are "on the house," thanks to student government. Other kinds of entertainment are also sponsored by student government. They are working on a speaker's series for the campus, hoping to be able to pull in some "big names," to attract student participation.

Student government is a big part of Orientation weekend, and as a part of that event, passes out free Central T-shirts to incoming freshmen. They also sponsor "Fair on the Square," which is an activity for the City of Fayette, but also promotes

---
[1] Material in this section taken from the interview with Martha Bradley, September 20, 2017

student involvement. Recent years have seen sponsored trips to St. Louis Cardinals' baseball games, with free tickets to the game and bus transportation provided.

In addition, the student government underwrites expenses for the campus radio and the Collegian newspaper. All of this is made possible because of a budget of approximately $180,000 a year, the source of which is student fees.

Greek Life

Fraternities, sororities, social clubs, whatever they are called, are an important part of college and university life. For some, membership is a status symbol. For others, membership means the opportunity to bond with men or women with whom one wants to be identified. Or the opportunity for social life with friends. At Homecoming in 2015, Alpha Phi Gamma (Mokers) celebrated their 70th year of existence at Central Methodist. One charter member returned to march in the parade with alumni and current members. He was asked "did you organize the fraternity because you wanted to bond with each other and this was a way to do that?" "No," he said, "we organized because of girls. The Navy was getting all the girls, and we thought if we were in a fraternity we'd have a better chance to get a date."[2] One more reason to join!

At the time of this writing, Central Methodist University has five fraternities and six sororities. Two of the fraternities, Tau Kappa Epsilon and Delta Beta Tau, are national. The other three – Alpha Phi Gamma, Chi Delta, and

---

[2] This was at a time when the V-12 program was still on campus and there were lots of sailors in training.

Phi Delta Theta, are local. Two sororities are also national – Delta Xi Nu and Kappa Beta Gamma. The others – Alpha Gamma Psi, Delta Pi Omega, Sigma Pi Alpha, and Zeta Psi Lambda – are local.

All are open to any student by invitation and all participate fully in the life of the campus. We have already noted that Alpha Phi Gamma celebrated 70 years of existence. A year later, Delta Pi Omega reached the same milestone. Phi Delta Theta began life as Sigma Alpha Chi in 1947, as a response to the creation of the Mokers. So they, too, have reached the 70th milestone. Zeta Psi Lambda is 57 years old at the time of this writing. Deeper digging revealed that Alpha Gamma Psi began life as Alpha Phi Alpha. They changed their name because of a name conflict with a national organization, but they have a 90 year history. But Chi Delta is the oldest group still in existence, tracing its origins back to the old Atom Club. Greek life has been an important part of Central Methodist for much of its history. It has brought improved social life to the campus, in terms of dances, parties, and other activities. It has sparked rivalries, intramural competition, and sometimes conflict, but always interest and added life to the campus.

Professional Fraternities and Clubs

There are 24 professional fraternities and clubs on the campus, 13 of whom are nationally affiliated. These range from honor societies, to leadership, to music, to groups affiliated with a specific course of study such as biology, chemistry, social science, math, and so on. Many students are involved in these groups. Some are open to anyone in a particular field, others are by invitation and/or grade standing. Participation in these organizations adds another layer of meaning to campus life.

In addition, there are 14 student organizations not related to any of the groups listed above. They include the Student Government Association, the Collegian (newspaper), theater groups, music groups, intramural athletics, and on and on.

Athletics

Central Methodist is a member of the National Association of Intercollegiate Athletics (NAIA) and the Heart of America Conference. Intercollegiate activities are important, and we'll return to them in more detail in a minute. But, first, we must acknowledge the importance of educating the whole person, which includes the physical well-being of students. The ancients had a phrase for it – "mens sana in corpore sana" – meaning "a sound mind in a sound body." Physical exercise, a sound body, is a key component of creating healthy, well-rounded persons. In addition, athletics contributes to the character-building which is a key component to a Central education. Teamwork, supporting each other on and off the field, co-operation are all part of a healthy character.

A third or more of the student body participates in intercollegiate sports.[3] There are, currently, 15 varsity programs and then junior varsity teams. These include football, baseball, men's basketball, women's basketball, men's cross-country, women's cross-country, men's golf, women's golf, men's soccer, women's soccer, men's track and field, women's track and field, softball, volleyball, and spirit squad. As of 2016, each football team in the conference gets

---
3 1997 Self-Study, p. 73

one home game and one away game on television. These games are shown on ESPN3, streaming on the internet only.

Title IX, of course, changed the face of intercollegiate athletics completely. Under that federal guideline, a school must have a women's sport for each sport for men. That's why, in the preceding paragraph, there is carefully listed both men and women's track and field, as well as softball for women balancing baseball for men, and so on.

One of the markers for the success of an athletic program is conference championships. For the period 1975 – 2016, Central Methodist had 32 conference championships, plus 20 times their athletic teams appeared in national tournaments, though they were not conference champions that particular year.[4] Conference championships were in baseball, football, volleyball, men's basketball, softball, both men's and women's track and field, women's basketball, sportsmanship, men's golf, and co-ed cheer. Most of those were repeated several times. Appearances in national tournaments were men's basketball, women's basketball, women's track, men's track, men's cross country, volleyball, dance, and cheer. Several of those sports appeared on the list more than once. More than once, teams were listed in the Sweet Sixteen, Elite Eight, or Final Four. In 2015, Central's Nick Homan was the national champion in the pole vault.

Another guide to the success of an athletic program is the number of All-Americans it produces over the years. Again, Central Methodist's program has impressive numbers. Since

---

[4] Data on championships, as well as on All-Americans, which follows in the next paragraph, are from CMU's athletic director, Brian Spielbauer.

the first All-American – Bob Iglehart in basketball, 1960 – there have been 159 All-Americans listed. The following sports produced All-Americans. Numbers in parentheses indicate the number of honorees in that sport.

- Men's basketball (12)
- Division 2 Football (5)
- Baseball (6)
- Women's Basketball (9)
- Men's Outdoor Track (25)
- Men's Indoor Track (28)
- Women's Outdoor Track (16)
- Women's Indoor Track (13)
- Softball (14, plus 1 Honorable Mention)
- Women's Cross Country (4)
- Men's Cross Country (2)
- Football (20, plus 2 Honorable Mentions)
- Volleyball (4)
- Men's Soccer (2)

It is clear that athletics not only provides the opportunity for building healthy bodies, it also provides the opportunity for national recognition for both the program and the individuals who participate in it.

In addition, there are club sports, those which are not official or coached. These teams do play other schools, however. The men's and women's flag football teams, for example, went to the state championships. The women's team won and played in the national tournament in Mississippi. The school provides some support, but only transportation and an athletic trainer. If a student wants an event, and students can get two teams together, the school supports it.

Intramural sports are just like they've always been – fun, pick-up games for people who want to be in athletics, but don't have time to practice at the varsity or junior varsity, probably not even the club level. Sports are important for physical health and for being a part of the university.

In many ways, student life is not so much a transformation as it is an evolution of how student life has always been organized at Central Methodist. In some other ways, student life fits the model of transformation as we have been using it in this book.

JOHN GOOCH

12

TRANSFORMING THE ALUMNI ASSOCIATION

The last decade of the old millennium and the first decade of the new millennium were times of fresh excitement and renewal for the Central Methodist Alumni Association. In the interests of full disclosure, I was a part of those changes, first as a member of the alumni board from about 1999 through 2006 and President of the Alumni Association from 2003-2005.

The changes began when the class agent program was formalized. Each graduating class had a representative whose role was to find ways to engage alumni with the college/university again. This program was limited to graduates of the Fayette campus, both because the extended locations were still taking form and because a way of relating to those graduates was being explored. The most important role of the class agent was to encourage classmates to return for Homecoming, to connect with the school and with each other in person again. Depending on the class and how hard the representatives worked at this, classes returned in greater or lesser numbers. Letters from the class agents said such things as, "wouldn't it be nice to see each other again before we die?" This was a particularly effective question for classes whose members were retired or nearing retirement. Younger classes worked more on the idea of reunion and catching up with old friends. Either way, alumni began to return in larger numbers.

For some alumni, that question was a clincher. They returned for Homecoming and were, indeed glad to see each other again. They also saw their alma mater with new eyes. Alumni began to see the needs of the college (as it was then) and also to see the potential for the future. There was the beginning of an excitement among alumni who returned, which laid the groundwork for closer relationships in the future. The administration supported this project not only with logistical help (mailings, etc.) but also with meetings with alumni. Particularly the honor classes each Homecoming were invited to a session with President Inman in which she highlighted the changes that were happening on campus and what new things were planned for the immediate future. Other alumni were also welcome to attend, but there was a special invitation for members of the honor classes. Responses to these sessions were remarks such as "Wow. I didn't know all that was happening." And, of course, there was a lot happening. This was also the era of refurbishing and renovating dormitories, planning for the Sesquicentennial and then celebrating it, looking forward to the demolishing of the Eyrie and the building of the new Student and Community Center.

Early in the 2000s, the Alumni Association Board appointed a sub-committee to rewrite the bylaws of the board to reflect the growing feeling about engagement with the future. One of the chief results of this rewrite was balanced class representation on the board. The new bylaws called for three members of the board from each decade (90s, 80s, 70s, etc., and each new decade). This brought a wider range of alumni to the board and some different perspectives on the relationships to the school. Particularly, that bylaw opened the door for engagement with older alumni, some even stretching back to the 1930s.

As we saw in an earlier chapter, the Alumni Association Board took a prominent role in the celebration of the Sesquicentennial. It must be said that there was room for more excitement. Homecomings for several years had been less than ideal. There was a lot of comment, most of it negative, about the parades. The floats were "not like we did them." The band was smaller than it had been in a long time, and this did not set well with alumni who remembered the large bands of their years at school and the memories of the "mud bowl" game in St. Louis which made the band famous nationally (Andy Warhol's fifteen minutes of fame). One does not know if these feelings were the beginning of the alumni band which participated in the Homecoming parades. We do know that the alumni band has grown over the years, until the 2016 edition overflowed their truck and included twirler alumni marching in front of the truck. It is also true that the Central band is again the large, exciting representative of the university. Go Eagles!

The Alumni Association was also active in gathering and displaying historical materials about the University.

For several years, the display of items was in a building just off the square owned by Jim Steele. The Board also had a tent outside the building where they offered coffee and donuts to alumni gathered for Homecoming. These displays of historical items proved so popular that, when the Student and Community Center (now the Inman Center) was finished, the Alumni Board arranged for display cases on the first floor for what is now the Living History Museum. Displays are now arranged by decades and are changed periodically.

For several years, on Homecoming weekend, there was a special alumni party held at Emmett's on the square. Classes that were celebrating significant anniversaries were especially invited, but all alumni were welcome. These events proved so popular that they outgrew the venue (as in, standing room only) and are now held at the historic Howard County Jail, just off the square.

And, for years, alumni events were blessed by the presence of Jim and Helen Thogmorton. "Dean T" and "Mrs. T" were always front and center at Homecoming, Alumni Weekend and other events involving alumni presence. They greeted all the alumni by name (they had more names in their heads than many alumni departments have on paper). They asked about jobs, children, other activities, and listened to the responses as if they were the most important news they had heard. For the Thogmortons, that was true – it was the most important conversation of the day. And so was the next one, and the next one. Those alumni who had come to Central out of some rural schools and were the first in their families to attend college remembered the Thogmortons as substitute parents who encouraged them through rough times in their adjustment. Those alumni who, as students, had to be reprimanded by Dean of Students James Thogmorton remembered him as one who cared, even while he was dealing with infractions of the rules. All the alumni I ever heard loved Jim and Helen. Which was good, because Jim and Helen loved them. And that relationship was a strong bond between the alumni and Central Methodist. Their deaths were a real blow to the Central family.

More recently, there were some misunderstandings between the alumni Association, on the one hand, and the Trustees and Administration on the other. The Association worked at helping Trustees and Administrators see that alumni loved the school. There had been "grumblings" from alumni that had raised questions in the minds of the powers that be, and it was important to communicate that those were concerns raised by alumni who loved the school and wanted it to be the best school in the state. One result of these conversations was the rescheduling of some events to open up channels of communication. For example, the Trustees now meet the same week as Alumni Weekend to provide more opportunities for mingling and conversation between the two groups. The relationship is now more open and welcoming for both alumni and trustees, which can only be a good thing for the university.

Alumni are crucial to the life of any college or university. In the case of Central Methodist, we now have some 17,000+ alumni (not counting the alumni of the extended campuses). That means 17,000+ people who represent the University in their vocations, their churches, and among prospective students. They are, whether they are aware of it, or not, our ambassadors. The task for the University is to keep up with them and help them keep up with the University. One way to do that is through print and mailings. Regular emails from the alumni office highlight specific themes each week.

In a more personal vein, there was a period in which University staff held regular alumni coffees in various locations around the state. These were simple get-togethers in a restaurant or coffee shop, where alumni gathered to renew relationships with each other and with the university. The staff person who was there from the University gave updates and other information about the school, but there was no pressure on alumni to do anything except relate. More "formal" gatherings have included alumni gatherings at the St. Louis Zoo, at Busch Stadium, and other venues. These are all aimed at strengthening connections between alumni and the University. David Hutchison, Executive Director of Advancement and Alumni Programs has said, "We create lasting opportunities to connect people's passions with the mission and vision of Central Methodist University." We do that in several ways. We listen to and learn from our alumni. We are friend-creators. We raise money for scholarships. We work capital funds campaigns.

The Alumni office staff at the University are clear about one thing. Central Methodist University does not want your money. Central Methodist University wants you. Money may be a part of that, but it is not even the most important part. That's a strong statement, but one that marks the work of those who work closely with alumni. Of course, Central Methodist needs your money, but if the only time you see anyone from the University, they are coming with their hand out, you soon won't answer their calls. If they come to build a relationship with you, you more likely will become an ambassador for the school. You'll be proud to display

Central pennants, etc., in your workplace. You'll support your church in raising scholarship funds, or recruiting students. You'll be a proud part of the Central family. It is fascinating to talk with alums at Homecoming or Alumni weekend. There is a pride in the University, an excitement about being back, a joy in greeting old friends. And, of course, all that helps to raise funds.

Another point to consider. The more alumni are connected, the more they add value to their degree. The stronger Central is, the more it is known in the state, the stronger relationships are with alumni, the more value the degree.

A special sub-set of alumni are those who began their college life at Central and then transferred to another school. Many of these still have a warm spot in their hearts for Central Methodist University. Some return for reunions at Homecoming, or for other special events. It is harder for the school to keep up with these alums, but progress is being made.

We noted earlier, in Chapter 8, that the alumni of the various extension campuses of the university do not have the same feeling of loyalty to the school that students from the Fayette campus do. This is understandable, because feelings of loyalty can be associated with specific places and events that are endemic to the Fayette campus. On the other hand, there could also be some feelings of gratitude to the school that made a baccalaureate degree possible from a distance that could translate into loyalty. The Alumni Board has wrestled with this question for over a decade, but has not been able to come up with a solution. This remains a challenge for the future.

13

CHRISTIAN HIGHER EDUCATION

This chapter is not about the history of the past few decades. It is not about ups and downs in enrollment or finances. Rather, it is about a dream. If Central Methodist University is a Christian institution, what kind of Christian is it? In this chapter, we will explore the idea of Christian higher education and how it is modeled on the Central campus. Not every reader of this chapter will agree with the model we describe here. But at least many readers will recognize in the model something of what they might have wished for themselves or what they would wish for their sons and daughters.

What is it that we're talking about when we say "Christian higher education"? Do we mean a system that strives for uniformity, that asks all the students and faculty and administration to believe in a certain way? Do we mean a system where the goal is to convert students and make them the same kind of Christians that we are? Do we mean a system that begins with a dogmatic view of, for example, the authority of the Bible, and demands that everyone adopt that view?

Or do we mean something entirely different? The model we are suggesting here is, indeed, something entirely different.

In 1996, the University Senate of the United Methodist Church put together a statement of what it means for an educational institution to be related to the church. Their work is worth quoting in full.[5]

> **Marks of a United Methodist-Related Institution**
>
> The University Senate of The United Methodist Church, an agency of General Conference, in 1996 affirmed marks of Church relationship which should be manifest in an institution meaningfully related to The United Methodist Church.
>
> 1. A Church-related institution identifies itself as such in printed materials, official listings, and other statements of self-description.
> 2. A Church-related institution identifies, respects, honors, and provides the teaching of religion and specifically, appropriate scholarly theological teaching in the Christian tradition within the curriculum.
> 3. A Church-related institution respects and honors religious practice and specifically, worship and service for students and faculty who choose to participate in the Christian tradition within the total life of the school.
> 4. A Church-related institution willingly allows faculty and students to explore the place in religious belief and practice, and specifically, the intellectual dimensions of Christian faith, in all academic

---

[5] "Marks of a United Methodist-Related Institution," The University Senate of the United Methodist Church, 1996

disciplines and co-curricular activities.
5. A Church-related institution encourages the exploration of the place of religious belief and practice in the larger society and advocates appropriate recognition of the contributions to public life.
6. A Church-related institution recognizes the Social Principles of the United Methodist Church and seeks to create a community of scholarship and learning which facilitates social justice.
7. A Church-related institution includes in its faculty, administrative officers, and board of trustees persons who understand and respect the relationship with the United Methodist Church.

Those seven points are not the final word on what makes higher education "Christian." But they open some windows through which we may glimpse some important truths. In reality, they are found on a poster which is displayed prominently in offices and on every bulletin board on the Central Methodist University campus. Note the stress on the intellect in Christian faith and on critical thinking and social justice.

In 2015, St. Louis University installed its first lay president. He was Jesuit-educated, as befits a Jesuit institution. What he said in an interview with *Universitas*, the alumni magazine, speaks directly to the question behind this chapter:

> The academy exists primarily for the discovery and transmission of knowledge. That's the "head" part of it. We're blessed with this amazing cognitive capacity and Jesuits are known for rigorously developing the tremendous gift of the human mind. We couple that intellectual rigor with an emphasis on the heart. We form people. As I said in my inaugural address, the mark of our alumni, the measure

of this institution, is not in the facts that are mastered, but in the character that is formed.[1]

Those words resonate with the mission statement of Central Methodist University, which says that the university "prepares students to make a difference in the world by emphasizing academic and professional excellence, ethical leadership, and social responsibility."[2]

Taken together, these three statements suggest that there is more to a Christian campus that expressing loyalty to doctrinal statements. That is not to say that doctrine is not important.

It is. But academic excellence is also important, and so is character-building. Cultural diversity is important for understanding, and living in, today's global village. So is an awareness of the global realities of our day. Another part of being a Christian campus is being engaged with the world locally.

So how does Central Methodist University measure up? Taking first the "Marks of a United Methodist-Related Institution":

1. Central proudly identifies itself as a United Methodist-related institution.
2. It does provide adequate scholarly teaching in the Christian tradition.
3. It does provide worship and service in the Christian tradition.
4. and 5. It does allow the free exploration of ideas in religious belief

---

[1] Laura Geiser, "Meet the President" in *Universitas*, Volume 41, Issue 1, Spring 2015

[2] Central Methodist University Overview, Fall 2015, p. 1

and practice.
6. It does seek to create a community of scholarship and learning which facilitates social justice.
7. Faculty, administrators and trustees understand and respect the relations with the United Methodist Church.

That takes care of playing by the "rules." But the "rules" seek the free expression of ideas and religious practice. What about how the rules work in daily life and practice on the campus and what that means for the growth in faith and service of the individual student?

In July of 2015, the Rev. Molly Moore became the Director of the Center for Faith and Service on the Central Methodist campus. Rev. Moore came from a background of 20 years in local churches, with a focus on spiritual formation.

An Associate Director and an Assistant Director came on board at the same time. The purpose of the Center is to educate and equip students to be faith-filled leaders of their communities. Note that this purpose is not to carry out a campus ministry program for the few years that students are in school. That ministry is important, but it is not an end in itself. The ultimate goal is to prepare students to become faithful leaders in the communities where they find themselves after graduation. That is, the goal is long-term. Specifically, the Center will "1) provide robust and inclusive campus ministry for students studying in Fayette; 2) strengthen the university's connection with the United Methodist Church, and 3) develop civic engagement opportunities for the entire campus community."[3] All three of these avenues will help equip students to become faithful

---
3 Central Methodist University Overview, Fall 2015, p. 7

(filled with faith) leaders in their communities.

Studies in brain development suggest that our brains are not ready to deal with abstract theological and philosophical ideas until (for most of us) we reach young adulthood. That means for ministry at the university level, reflection on faith and life is critically important. What is our faith? Who is God? What does it mean to say that Jesus is the Son of God? What is our faith tradition? What does our faith teach us about how to engage with real issues in the world? How does what we say in worship (reciting the Creed, for example) relate to our daily life? Questions like those are being asked by students as they try to understand who they are, what they believe, and what their lives mean. How they find answers to those questions are crucial for their lives – and a key part of any kind of Christian ministry on the campus.

So how do those words play out in the lives of students? First, there is time to worship and reflect. Central Methodist provides a voluntary weekly chapel service, with strong student leadership. Students lead the service and reflect on faith and life. There is a good-sized praise band, whose music supports and enhances the worship. Evidence of administrative support for the service is seen in the fact that President Drake often attends, and sometimes plays keyboard with the band. Other administrators and faculty are also present for the services, and their example of faith provides a model for students. I had the opportunity to attend a chapel service recently, and the campus community filled Linn Memorial Church.

There is an emphasis on character formation in the total picture of campus life. Remember what the President of St. Louis University said, "We form people....the measure of this institution is not in the facts that are mastered, but in the character that is formed." Character formation plays a significant role in the curriculum, and it also appears here in worship. Students are challenged to discover who they are and what their lives can mean.

There is an emphasis on service learning. This is the civic engagement component of the Center's purposes. On the one hand, students take the knowledge they learn in the classroom and convert that knowledge to wisdom through serving others. On the other hand, service learning is more than just lending a helping hand. The "learning" component is reflecting on what they learn from the servant experience and sharing that learning with others. For example, a group of students might take on a project to help a senior citizen with yard work, cleaning, minor repairs on the house. That's service. Service learning is reflecting on what they did and why – "Why is it that older people sometimes need that kind of help? What does it say about our society? How do I feel about having participated in the project? What difference did it make that several of us worked together? What does the project have to do with my relationships with others and with God?" Another group might work at the local food pantry, stocking shelves, filling backpacks for children who would otherwise not have a good meal over the weekend. That's the service. The learning component comes in knowing that people are hungry, and asking questions such as, "Why, in the richest nation in the history of the world, do we have children who are perpetually hungry? What does that say about the way we deal with hunger and poverty? What does our faith have to say about that? What, for instance, did Jesus say about feeding the hungry?

Or Moses, or Mohammed, or the Buddha? What do our traditions teach us? What would St. Francis of Assisi say to us? Or Dr. Martin Luther King? Or the Dalai Lama? Or other faithful persons who have gone before us?" That is service learning.

The most recent service day (with classes dismissed – this is important) had 830 participants, students and faculty, who worked at 50 different sites, and contributed 2,213.5 hours of service. Reflection on the service day happened in the classrooms in the following days.

One needs to think about the faith. There is an intellectual component to faith. A part of the wisdom in the Christian tradition comes from the Middle Ages (of all places!) where it was understood that Christians would not long hold to a faith that they could not rationally defend, at least to themselves. In the Middle Ages that wisdom applied primarily to a literate minority. Today we assume wide-spread literacy, but the wisdom still holds. One of the great blessings of the United Methodist Church is that "you don't have to check your brains at the door." University students are thinking about faith and life – structured opportunities to share thoughts and questions both encourage the process and build in tools for engaging in it. On several occasions, I've been on the campus and seen signs advertising a gathering for asking hard questions. Christian higher education should always involve dealing with the hard questions, whether there are answers that come easily or not. Critical thinking is an important component of faith.

Does this fully answer the question about what makes Christian higher education Christian? Probably not. One hopes, however, that it does set out some of the marks of an institution that is as concerned about building a life as it is about teaching facts. If a student at Central Methodist grows in his or her understanding of self, if he or she has learned to struggle with the hard questions, if he or she has participated in service learning and discovered how to reflect on life experience in relationship to her or his faith in God, then we can say that the university experience has been a Christian one. If, in addition, he or she has learned about religious diversity in a complex world, if he or she has come to some understanding of the meaning of faith, then we can say with certainty that it has been a Christian experience.

14

CENTRAL METHODIST AND THE CHURCH

There is a trend.[1] Each new President of the University, as he or she takes office, hears that the relationship with the church is not good. The church, in this case, is the Annual Conference (or Conferences, before 2000) of the United Methodist Church in Missouri. Each President then reports in later years that the relationship is much better. Then he or she retires, a new President comes in and learns that the relationship with the church is not good. There must be an evil genie that destroys the relationship between University and Church during the transition period between Presidents!

There have, in fact, been times when that relationship was not all that cordial, no matter how the University and the Conference might have wished differently. Or the relationship

---

[1] This chapter applies primarily to the Fayette campus. The locations at community colleges and other sites do not have the relationship to the United Methodist Church that the core campus has.

with the churches of the Conference was good, but not with the Conference leadership. But, for the most part, University and Church have moved along together, even in times when one or both might have wished for a better relationship.

One of the tensions in the relationship is financial. The Annual Conference gives money to Central Methodist University each year. For years, that took the form of an apportionment, which is a budget line item for each local church. Some churches did not pay that apportionment, and the total given to Central suffered as a result. There were a variety of reasons why a church might not pay its apportionment. One would be that there was simply not enough income in that congregation to meet all their apportionments. Another would be that the church was unhappy with the school for some reason. In recent years, that apportionment has been changed to an "asking," or suggested donation. Since that was instituted, income from the Conference has dropped drastically (see Chapter 5 for details). Congregations continue to ask: what are we getting for our money? OR we don't see any benefit to our church from the University. Why should we give our money to it?

One reason for giving is that Central Methodist University trains leaders for the church. United Methodist alumni include bishops, district superintendents, pastors, music leaders, lay leaders of the conference and the local church, judges, doctors, teachers, parents, the list could go on and on. Local congregations often take that kind of leadership for granted, without reflecting on how those leaders were educated and by whom.

Central Methodist University's mission reflects the

same fundamental values of The United Methodist Church of which it is a part. The school intends to prepare students for lifelong learning, social responsibility, and service. We saw that in greater detail in Chapter Two. Those values are stressed throughout the campus experience, and the college-church relationship makes possible an engagement with values, mission, people and service in a way that state schools cannot.[2]

Let's remember that Central was founded by two Southern Methodist preachers, Nathan Scarritt and David Rice McAnally. It was intended to be the only Methodist "literary institution of the highest order in Missouri."[3] Today, the strategic planning process has helped us realize that the church relationship is our defining distinction.[4] The church relationship defines the central character of the University and led to its designation by the John Templeton Foundation as one of only 134 "character building" colleges in the United States.

From the beginning, Central's identification was with the Methodist Church (and its successor bodies). The founders intended that it should be the only Methodist college in the state, so that it could be a strong focus for the church. Throughout the history of Methodism in Missouri, there have been many other Methodist educational institutions founded.[5]

---

2 Central Methodist College, 1997 Self-Study, p. 31

3 Frank C. Tucker, *Central Methodist College, 110 Years*. Nashville: Parthenon Press, ssss, pp. 15-16

4 Central Methodist College, 1997 Self-Study, p, 30

5 These include: Avalon Academy (Avalon), Bellevue Collegiate Institute (Caledonia), Carleton\ Institute (St. Francois County), Central Female

Many of them simply closed in the course of time, such as the Bellevue Collegiate Institute. Others merged with other colleges, often out of state. For example, George R. Smith College was merged into Philander Smith College in Little Rock, Arkansas. Missouri Wesleyan merged with Baker University of Ballwin City, Kansas, around 1928. Scarritt Bible School moved to Nashville in 1924. Still others found new life as part of the university system of the State of Missouri. Lincoln and Lee University, for example, is now known as the University of Missouri – Kansas City. Maryville Seminary operates as Northwest Missouri State University. And, finally, Cottey College was sold to the P.E.O. in 1927, and continues in existence today under their auspices.

So – United Methodist identity is one of CMU's distinctions. We are a part of the church, and proud of it. This is highlighted in the statements of values, mission, and goals. For years, the President of the college was required

College (Lexington) Central Wesleyan College (Warrenton), Cottey College (Nevada), Danville Female Academy (Danville, George R. Smith College (Sedalia), Howard Payne College (Fayette), Johnson College(Macon), Kansas City National Training School for Deaconesses and Missionaries(Kansas City), Kansas City University (Kansas City), Lewis College (Glasgow), Lincoln and Lee University (Kansas City), Marionville College (Marionville), Marthasville Seminary (Marthasville), Marvin Collegiate Institute (Fredericktown), Maryville Seminary (Maryville), Missouri Wesleyan College (Cameron), Morrisville Collegiate Institute (Morrisville), Northwest Missouri College (Albany), Scarritt Bible and Training School (Kansas City), Scarritt Collegiate Institute,(Neosho), St. Charles College (St. Charles). Source is institutions of Higher Education, United Methodist Church, Missouri." A resource provided by the Commission on Archives and History, the Missouri Conference, The United Methodist Church. n.d., n.p.

to be a Methodist minister. Not until the end of the 20th century was this tradition broken, and lay persons could become the head of the school.

The University works to strengthen this relationship by frequent visits to local churches by the President, musical groups, and others. One of the challenges of the relationship is the staffing of visits to 972 churches.[6] Visits are reinforced by mailings, email postings, and as many other forms of communication as possible.

Bishop Ann Sherer said that Central Methodist College is the college most closely related to the church of those with which she has worked. Bishop Sherer was active in her relationship with the Board of Trustees, and even made it to one or two meetings of the Alumni Board. Bishop Schnase was almost always represented at the Trustees meetings, but seldom was there in person. One Trustee said that Central was not a problem for Bishop Schnase, so he left it alone and concentrated on the problems that need to be dealt with. That is an understandable attitude. Preachers, business executives, and other leaders all do that. The "squeaky wheel," the department that is a problem, gets the attention.

In practical terms, some 18% of Central's student body on the Fayette campus are United Methodists (Church affiliation figures for students in the extended campuses are not available.). United Methodist students receive half tuition scholarships, simply because of their church affiliation. One of the goals for the future might well be to increase the percentage of United Methodist students on the Fayette campus.

---

6 Central Methodist College Self-Study Report 1997-1998 Strategic Planning Conclusions, p. 3

15
Transforming Students

Changes in the buildings on campus are important. It's important that the University is in good financial condition. But the most important thing about Central Methodist University is the transformation in the lives of students. What happens to young people when they come to Fayette to get an education? There are dozens of stories that could be told. The ones in this chapter are representative of the changes in the lives of so many youth who come to Central. Note that this chapter is not so much about how the broad picture of Central Methodist has been transformed in recent years. Rather, it is about how individual student's lives have been changed – transformed – as a result of their Central experience. This has always been true at Central. The key to the existence of the school is how student's lives are changed.

The most moving story I heard was from a CMU freshman named Ammie Akzam. She shared it with a group of alumni and other members of the 1854 Society, and it has been printed and mailed to many others. It is so important to the way that Central's mission plays out in the lives of people that we share it here once again.

"My name is Ammie Akzam and I am a freshman at CMU. My family and I moved quite a bit while living in California as a child, then Texas, and finally Missouri. During those years, I had to take on the role of taking care of my siblings and always doing the adult thing, because I didn't really have adult parents in my life. My way of escaping my not so great life was school. School was my safe ground, along with my church community. As a child I wanted to do many things I knew I wasn't able to do because my family wasn't able to fund those things, but that didn't stop me from trying. I went through many things in life, but I kept my head strong and focused on what I really wanted in life.

"My dad bounced from job to job, and sometimes we had to live off my parents' SSI checks; we were the definition of worthless poor people. This is not what I wanted my life to ever be like. This wasn't my definition of HOME. We eventually had to move back to California and through that time I struggled being myself, I was becoming a failure. Then, in January of 2012, my dad died of a heart attack. It was the worst thing that had ever happened to me. We may not have been close, but he was my father and had tried to provide for us. When it happened, the first person I called was Sue Bachman, the wife of a couple at my church back in Chillicothe, who had really been influential in my life there. I struggled with what my new life was going to be like until one day Sue called me and asked me if I wanted to come live with her and Scott in Missouri. Everything changed after they became my guardians, and gave me a true home – which is all I ever wanted.

"As I started to think about college, I visited several schools, such as Missouri State and also CMU. I knew that I wanted to be a teacher, my passion for it was real. MSU had a great campus and plenty to do, but when I stepped on campus at CMU my eyes lit up and right then and there I fell in love with the beauty of the campus. The faculty and staff were nice. I felt as if I was at home. I knew this was the place for me. I wanted a place to call HOME. That is why I chose Central Methodist. CMU is my home now and I am grateful to be a part of a college like this. Central has many great people that make CMU the best place to be. I would like to thank all of them for letting me be a part of it. I am proud to be an Eagle!

"I love my new HOME. Once I graduate from CMU I plan to have my bachelor's degree in elementary education. I hope to obtain a job at an elementary school somewhere. I want to teach for as long as I can. Being here at CMU means that I have been given the opportunity to succeed in my passion. CMU is where my life is starting and it has become an enabler to pursue my passion in life. CMU has given me a new family, and home."[1]

Note some key words in that statement. "The definition of worthless"; "I was becoming a failure"; and the contrast to "CMU is where my life is starting;" "It has become an enabler to pursue my passion in life." That's a real transformation. Central was not the only enabler, but certainly Central was a key part of Ammie's transformation to a new family, a new home. She was transformed as a result of her Central experience.

"Family" is a word that appears in the witness of both

---
[1] This material courtesy of Central Methodist University

students and alumni. A 2014 graduate wrote "My freshman year at CMU I didn't know anyone, but I gained an entire family by the end of my schooling."[2] And a 2009 graduate wrote "(faculty) whose character and compassion for not just teaching students, but inspiring us to be learners and thinkers for purposes much greater than ourselves greatly impacted my vision for the future. CMU gave me much more than a degree...I gained a vision and the necessary tools to achieve my dreams."[3]

It seems clear that an institution that takes its mission and vision seriously, that lives it out in teaching and interaction with individuals, can indeed transform those individuals to become the leaders of tomorrow.

And then there is Danielle Franklin.

"My name is Danielle Mae Franklin and I graduated from Central Methodist University on May 13th of this year (2017). I first decided to attend Central when I was in 8th grade visiting for the joyous event of Music Fest. I spent the day running around, singing, and playing the clarinet with my classmates and at the end of the day, I looked over at my mom and said, 'this is where I wanna go to college.'

"One year after that, my dad left us. I didn't think that I would be able to attend college anymore. I was going to be a first generation student, but I knew that we wouldn't have the funds to get me through. I still got good grades and was active in extracurricular activities, but I didn't think I would be attending college.

"Two years later, I attended Junior Day and applied

---

2 Julie (Ramiso) Massana '14 *Talon*, Spring 2015

3 Seth Baumann, '09 *Talon*, Spring 2016

at Central. I didn't actually realize that I was applying at first, I just wanted the cool, free t-shirt. I got my acceptance letter in September of my senior year, came in October for a one-on-one visit, and fell even more in love with the photogenic campus and the community that is embedded it. In February, I auditioned for a Choir and Theater scholarship – excited that I could still be part of organizations that I loved throughout middle and high school. I was awarded the President's Scholarship as well as a Hall of Sponsors Scholarship.

"The last four years I have been active in Conservatory Singers, Sigma Tau Delta Mu Lambda Chapter International English Honor Society, and local social sorority Alpha Gamma Psi. I have been honored for my grades and leadership with being inducted in to the Top 10% Freshmen Class Honor Society Alpha Lambda Delta, Leadership Society Omicron Delta Kappa, and inducted into the Top 10% of the 2017 Graduating Class Sigma Epsilon Pi. This year alone I was editor of the CMU Literary Magazine Inscape, President of the Sigma Tau Delta Chapter, Alumnae Secretary and Fundraising Chair for Alpha Gamma Psi, nominated and elected Homecoming Queen, and I passed my Honors Thesis Defense with no revisions.

"While pursuing my Bachelor's in English I have been given many opportunities to help my writing grow and improve. Working as a Student Resource Assistant at the Career Development Center under Nicolette Yevich I have written Semester Stories on the work being done at the Career Center for the Talon and for the Collegian. I have been part of the Student Alumni Ambassador Board where I've helped with events and getting current students more involved and giving them opportunities to make connections with alums. I have been editor of Inscape for two years, and I had an internship under Dr. Kevin Carnahan as an Undergraduate Editorial Assistant for his new book, and for the *Journal of the Society of Christian Ethics*.

"I have had the wonderful opportunity to be consistently involved with the campus and different activities that engage with all of my interests here at Central. Opportunities that I would not have had anywhere else. If it was not for the support of generous donations from people like you, I would not have been able to attend this wonderful institution and graduate with Honors in my Degree. Thank you so much!"[4]

Part of Danielle's transformation was the financial help that made it possible for her to become a part of the Central Methodist family. What a great success she has been at Central, and what a witness she will become to the larger community wherever she finds herself!

One more: "I came to Central Methodist to play soccer and earn a criminal justice degree. My world was rocked when I took a criminal justice introductory class and realized it wasn't a good fit for me. Luckily, I have a great advisor who encouraged me to take my time choosing a major and to enroll in more introductory classes to learn about different fields. Introduction to Nursing was engaging and fun from the very beginning. The new Thogmorton Center for Allied Health provides a hands-on learning environment where I tend to learn at my best."[5]

These students and many more like them, have been

---
[4] This material courtesy of Central Methodist University.

[5] Katie Bloodworth, '19, courtesy of Central Methodist University.

transformed by being a part of the Central Methodist family. They are the result of all the other transformations we've seen throughout this book. They are the reason that the rest of the Central family continues its support.

16

Transition to the Future

The Year of our Lord 2013 – the end of an era at Central Methodist University. Dr. Inman retired. So what did her 18 years at Central Methodist mean for the University? What did she accomplish?

I began the research for this book by asking Dr. Inman, "When Methodist preachers move, they often say about the church they left, 'I did these three things while I was their pastor.' I'm asking you the same thing. What three things did you accomplish as President of Central Methodist?"

She answered that question by pushing the envelope, as she did in so many areas while she was President. First, she said, was the renaissance of Central Methodist University: program focus, state-of-the-art information technology, online courses and programs, Fayette campus transformation through renovation and new construction, emphasis on growth with quality, fiscal responsibility (shift from annual operating deficits to substantial excesses of revenues over expenses).

Second was "I taught the institution to fly (soar): nimble, entrepreneurial, market-oriented; shift from "How do we keep the doors open?" to "What strategic initiative shall we undertake next?" (OR: "What doors do we want next to open?")

Third was the emphasis on strong constituent relationships: partner institutions and communities (formal partnerships with all 13 of Missouri's two-year public institutions as well as more than 100 high schools through dual credit), higher education environment – among both public and private institutions, the Higher Learning Commission (regional accrediting agency), the Missouri Annual Conference and local United Methodist churches, statewide mission and presence, alumni, and donors.

These things were accomplished, she said, through the growth and development of the Board of Trustees, first-rate senior staff of breakthrough people, developing and following strategic and master plans, including clear, concise statements of mission, vision, values, and educational goals; transparent, inclusive leadership style and open book management; and enhanced fundraising, enrollment growth (six times), increase (three times) in operating budget and endowment.

The "envelope pushing" on the assignment she was given came shortly after the first answer to the question, when I received three more statements of what she saw as her legacy. These were, first, the name change from college to university (2004) reflected both our statewide presence and the addition of graduate programs.

Second, she added the word "responsibilities" to the

degree conferring proclamation: "By the power and authority vested in me by the State of Missouri and the Board of Trustees of Central Methodist University, I hereby confer upon you the degree…, with all the rights, honors, privileges, and responsibilities appertaining thereto." This was important as our mission includes the word and concept of "responsibility" – emphasizing to the graduates the importance of giving as well as receiving.

Third, the completion of three capital campaigns (exceeding the goal in each case). The Campaign for Central at $35.8 million was the largest in Central's history and demonstrated Central's renewed ability to raise significant funds for significant projects. This success shifted people's focus from "you think you're going to do it THIS time?" to asking "What's next?" (The "it" in the first question referred to building a student center, which had been discussed and even designed at least twice earlier.)

We have seen, throughout the book, how each of these (two sets of) three accomplishments occurred and transformed some part of Central Methodist, joining with other accomplishments to create a transformed whole. Obviously, they were not accomplished single-handedly, as President Inman was the first to admit. Trustees, staff, alumni, and other groups played a role, as we have seen. But they also could not have happened without the vision and drive that President Inman brought to the University.

Lest we think that the above material be self-serving, we need to take a look at what the General Board of Higher Education and Ministry of the United Methodist Church had to say about some of the results of President Inman's tenure.

1. Nearly five-fold increase in enrollment, to almost 5300 last fall
2. Completion of three capital campaigns, netting the University nearly $50 million.
3. A near tripling of the University endowment, to $31 million.
4. Growth in CMU operating revenues from $8.5 million when she arrived to more than $26 million this past year.
5. Campus improvements totaling in excess of $50 million.[1]

Another listing included technology upgrades to the campus, the expansion of CGES, the increase in the size of the Board of Trustees, the name change to University, and the development of new programs of study. We have seen all of those reflected in earlier chapters of this book.

President Inman did not confine her efforts to the campus. In 2012, she was invited by the Commissioner of Higher Education of the State of Missouri to join him and four other persons to help develop a strategic plan for higher education in the state in response to the governor's stated goal of 60% college degree attainment by 2025. This was not only an honor, but also a tall order since Missouri was currently at 32% and the national average was only 39%.[2] However, there was definitely room for improvement.

In the spring of 2009, the Talon reported that Dr. Inman had been elected President of the University Senate of the United Methodist Church. This is the oversight body for the schools and colleges related to the United Methodist Church. That same issue reported that Inman was the Past President

---

[1] The General Board of Higher Education and Ministry, The United Methodist Church. n.p., n.d.

[2] Minutes of the Board of Trustees meeting, February 17 and 18, 2012

of the Independent Colleges and Universities of Missouri, and is the Chair of the Board of the Missouri Humanities Council. She is also Chair of the Presidential Advisory Committee for the Missouri Coordinating Board for Higher Education. She also serves on the Board of the Great Rivers Council of Boy Scouts and contributed to the President's Commission on Foreign Language and International Studies. She was also selected as a Kellogg Foundation National Fellow.

Dr. Inman was honored as the Business Leader of the Year 2008 by the Fayette Rotary Club. The award is given annually to outstanding business and community leaders in Fayette, and is voted on by the members of the club.[3]

In addition, President Inman engaged in her favorite leisure pastime, community theater. Her starring in "Love Letters," opposite Emeritus Professor Dr. Joseph Geist, was a treat long to be remembered. She was active in Fayette community events, Linn Memorial United Methodist Church, and preached most Sundays in a United Methodist Church somewhere in Missouri.

When President Inman announced her intention to retire, the Trustees sprang into motion to secure a successor who could build on the strengths of the past 18 years and lead Central Methodist University into a continued future of success. There were three candidates in the final interview.[4] The consensus after the interview with Roger Drake was to recommend him to the Board. The committee was not a quorum of the Board, and they had to have a vote quickly

---

3 *Talon*, Spring 2009, p. 10

4 The information in this paragraph comes from the interview with former Trustee Chair Glenn Cox, on July 18, 2016

because Dr. Drake had an offer from another Methodist school in Kansas. Glenn Cox and Tad Perry got on the phones and started calling Trustees. That way, they were able to get a majority vote for Dr. Drake.

In Dr. Drake's words, the transition was glorious. President Inman graciously shared her knowledge and information. She left behind a strong leadership team. She continued to work with certain donors to get them moved over into relationship with the new President. She spoke at the inauguration, at baccalaureate and the dedication of the "Family Tree" sculpture in the sculpture park outside Classic Hall. She continues to be a generous donor to the University. Central is "home" to the Inmans, as it is to so many alumni. In retirement in Georgetown, Texas, President Inman has become a Trustee of Garrett/Evangelical Theological Seminary, one of the great theological schools of United Methodism. She continues to celebrate her love for community theater.

When asked what gifts and graces he brought to Central Methodist, Dr. Drake replied that he believed he was a transformational agent, an entrepreneur, and that he was an analytical thinker and planner. He is a President who came to Central from the business side of higher education. One early comment was "Dr. Inman was a scholar, I'm a bean-counter." Certainly he is more than that, but the business background is certainly a plus. Dr. Drake also says he believes in calculated risk, which is also a plus in today's context of higher education.

For him, the beauty of Central Methodist is that the President can be the kind of leader he/she needs to be.

Inherent in the situation at Central is an arsenal of the tools the school needs to change itself if it needs to.

Challenges for the Future

Certainly a big challenge is affordability. Central Methodist is enrollment driven. Without students, the school would die. In the present context of higher education, public institutions have over-reached. They are the competition for private schools, and that means the appeal to students and the financial situation of those private schools is not good. Central, however, has branding, destination courses, quality, character building. Central is in a position to meet those challenges in ways that other private liberal arts colleges in Missouri are not.

So, while perhaps the biggest challenges in Central's history lie ahead of us, there is also the sense that our best days are also ahead of us.

Playing With the Big Kids

ABOUT THE PRESS

Eagle Heights Press, a division of *Eagle Heights LLC.*, publishes thriller, fantasy, science fiction, historical fiction, paranormal romance, speculative fiction, young adult, non-fiction, and more.

Find us on the web at eagleheightspress.com.

www.ingramcontent.com/pod-product-compliance
Lightning Source LLC
Chambersburg PA
CBHW042045280426
43661CB00094B/1039